D1402461

YA
973.312 Morgan, David T.
M821   North Carolinians in the
          Continental Congress/

305988

DEMCO

north carolinians in the continental congress

north carolinians in the continental congress

By DAVID T. MORGAN and
WILLIAM J. SCHMIDT

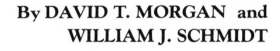

JOHN F. BLAIR, Publisher
Winston-Salem, North Carolina

LIBRARY
WAYNE STATE COLLEGE
WAYNE, NEBRASKA

Copyright © 1976 by JOHN F. BLAIR, Publisher
Library of Congress Catalog Card Number: 76–40113
ISBN 0–910244–89–8
All rights reserved
Printed in the United States of America

Illustration Credits

The author is indebted to the following for kind permission to use photographs and drawings:
Independence National Historical Park Collection 11
Library of Congress 8–9, 87
National Portrait Gallery of London 91
North Carolina Division of Archives and History ii–iii, 2, 6, 15, 21, 23, 29, 31, 33, 34, 41, 43, 54, 56, 59, 60, 64, 72, 76, 80–81, 88
North Carolina Division of Travel and Promotion 22

Library of Congress Cataloging in Publication Data

Morgan, David T
   North Carolinians in the Continental Congress.

   Bibliography: p.
   Includes index.
   SUMMARY: Discusses North Carolina's involvement in the Continental Congress and the American Revolution.
   1. United States. Continental Congress. 2. North Carolina—Politics and government—Revolution, 1775–1783. [1. United States. Continental Congress. 2. North Carolina—Politics and government—Revolution, 1775–1783] I. Schmidt, William J., 1929–   joint author. II. Title.
E303.M87   973.3'12   76–40113
ISBN 0–910244–89–8

acknowledgments

THE AUTHORS are indebted to many people. Unfortunately, we cannot single out all who have helped in one way or another. However, special thanks are due to those who have made particular contributions to our work.

First, we wish to thank the *North Carolina Historical Review* for permission to reprint portions of two articles, written respectively by both and by one of the authors and published in that journal. Second, we are grateful to the College of Liberal Arts of Texas A&M University for a grant from the Dean's Discretionary Fund, which made some of our research possible. Dr. F. W. R. Hubert, now dean of the College of Education, was dean of the College of Liberal Arts when the grant was made in 1969. Third, we both owe a great deal to Professor Hugh T. Lefler, that great man of North Carolina history, who guided us through numerous research projects—some of which led to this book.

D. T. M and W. J. S.

May, 1976

305988

contents

Introduction   ix

Chapter

  1 Faraway Philadelphia: An Introduction   3

  2 From Resistance to Revolution: 1774–1776   17

  3 The Confederation   35

  4 Men, Money, and Materiel for War   50

  5 Trying to Turn Land into Money   71

  6 The Long Search for Peace   84

  7 The North Carolina Delegates: An Evaluation   96

Appendix

  I The Declaration of Independence   111

  II The Constitution of North Carolina, 1776   116

  III The Articles of Confederation   126

  IV The Treaty of Paris, 1783   136

Bibliography   141

Index   145

introduction

THIS IS THE STORY of the North Carolinians who served in the Continental Congress between 1774 and 1789, including the years of the Revolutionary War. Oddly enough, it is a story that has never been told in a single work but has been scattered in original documents, general histories, and articles in periodicals.

The organization used in this work is both chronological and topical, the first three chapters being largely chronological and the last four largely topical. To acquaint the reader at the outset with the names of all seventeen delegates (including the ones who played an insignificant part in the story), the authors offer the following list, giving the names and years (or parts of years) in which the delegates served:

1.	Blount, William	1782–1783, 1786–1787
2.	Burke, Thomas	1777–1781
3.	Caswell, Richard	1774–1775
4.	Harnett, Cornelius	1777–1779
5.	Hawkins, Benjamin	1782–1783, 1787
6.	Hewes, Joseph	1774–1777, 1779
7.	Hill, Whitmel	1778–1780
8.	Hooper, William	1774–1777
9.	Johnston, Samuel	1780–1781
10.	Jones, Allen	1779–1780
11.	Jones, Willie	1780

12. Nash, Abner   1782–1783
13. Penn, John   1775–1780
14. Sharpe, William   1779–1781
15. Spaight, Richard Dobbs   1783–1785
16. Williams, John   1778
17. Williamson, Hugh   1782–1785, 1787–1789

These men were chosen at first by the revolutionary provincial congresses, of which five were called sporadically in North Carolina between August, 1774, and December, 1776. The Fifth Provincial Congress, meeting in Halifax during the last two months of 1776, gave North Carolina its first state constitution. That document, among other things, created a legislature or "General Assembly," which henceforth elected the new state's delegates to the Continental Congress for one-year terms. Once elected, the delegates were answerable to and paid by the Assembly.

The missions of the seventeen congressmen varied with changing circumstances. Those who served before July, 1776, were in Congress to cooperate with the representatives of the other colonies in adopting measures designed to force a change in British colonial policy and restore harmony between the colonies and the mother country. After the Declaration of Independence, the North Carolina delegates were there to cope with the problems of independence and to protect the interests of North Carolina in any union that might be formed by the now "free and independent States." Whether they served before or after the Declaration of Independence, the men who represented North Carolina could accomplish their mission in various ways: by offering ideas, by engaging in debates, by doing tedious committee work, and by serving on the executive boards created to solve "national" political, economic, and military problems. What the delegates did and how well they did it is the subject of the pages that follow.

north carolinians in the continental congress

William Hoope.

Richard Caswell

Joseph Hewes

1

faraway philadelphia: an introduction

EXACTLY ONE YEAR before the first major battle of the Revolutionary War at Bunker Hill, the Massachusetts legislature, on June 17, 1774, called upon the "several Colonies on this Continent" to send delegates to an intercolonial congress in Philadelphia in September. In Massachusetts, and in other colonies, many felt that Great Britain's colonial policy was becoming increasingly repressive. The recently passed Coercive Acts were causing anger in America, and the intercolonial meeting would be an opportunity to work out a unified response to Britain's alarming colonial policies.

When North Carolina's royal governor, Josiah Martin, heard of the impending congress, he made up his mind not to call the colony's provincial assembly into session in time to elect delegates to the Philadelphia meeting. Angered by the governor's tactics, some of the province's political leaders, including John Harvey, Cornelius Harnett, and William Hooper, demanded that an extralegal "provincial congress independent of the governor" be elected to meet in New Bern on August 25. On the appointed day, seventy-one elected delegates appeared from thirty of the thirty-six counties and four of the six borough towns and remained in session for three days. Among other business, the provincial delegates chose from among themselves William Hooper, Richard Caswell, and Joseph Hewes to go to Philadelphia that autumn and represent North Carolina at what would later be called the First Continental Congress. No one could foresee that this called meeting would eventually become a permanent part of a national political system that would require having representatives present on a full-time basis.

In North Carolina, during the next few years, as the need arose, other provincial congresses were called, elected, and convened—one in New Bern, one in Hillsborough, and two in Halifax. The Third (or Hillsborough) Provincial Congress established for the province a provisional government, which continued the periodic meetings of a congress and created a thirteen-member provincial council to handle executive and administrative matters, as well as instituting local committees of safety to organize resistance against the British. The Fifth Provincial Congress produced the state constitution of 1776.

Until this time the men sent as North Carolina's delegates to the Continental Congress were also delegates to the provincial congresses. They served one-year terms in Philadelphia and were answerable to and paid by authority of the provincial congresses. When the new state constitution went into effect in 1777, the General Assembly elected and paid the congressional representatives, who were sometimes members of the state legislative body as well. Until 1778 North Carolina chose to send only three delegates to Congress each year, even though some of the other provinces sent larger delegations. As long as North Carolina had at least one delegate present, its interests could be protected because each state had only one vote until the present Constitution was operative in 1789. With such a small delegation, however, North Carolina risked being unrepresented if illness or pressing personal business kept all three men from their duties. In 1778 the General Assembly increased the number of delegates to five, requiring that three be present at all times. The Articles of Confederation allowed each state to have as many as seven delegates; to be represented by an even number could be a disadvantage under the Articles for a state lost its vote if its delegates were evenly divided on an issue. In 1779 North Carolina named six delegates, but never, during the war years, had a larger delegation.

William Hooper, Joseph Hewes, and Richard Caswell pleased the North Carolina Provincial Congress with their service during the First Continental Congress and were again sent to Philadelphia in the spring of 1775. Their renewed appointment to Congress was a mark of honor, but all three men came to have second thoughts about serving when it became apparent to them that the Continental Congress would probably be in session indefinitely. Remaining far from home in Philadelphia, month after month, was a most displeasing prospect.

The first to become disenchanted was Richard Caswell. Forty-six years old in 1775, he was one of North Carolina's most prominent slaveholding planters. A Marylander by birth, he had come to North Carolina in 1752 and had settled in Johnston County by 1754. He had been a highly respected and popular legislator in the provincial assembly since 1754. In Philadelphia, however, he was scarcely noticed during the First Continental Congress. Nor would he receive much attention during the short time he would serve in the Second Congress. His failure to make significant contributions to the deliberations and the distastefulness of being so far from home for long periods were probably the main factors in his decision to leave Congress.

Hooper was the ablest of the first three North Carolina delegates and the man with the most impressive background. Born in Boston and educated at Harvard, he had studied law with the famous James Otis before moving to North Carolina and settling near Wilmington in 1767. Becoming quite successful as a lawyer, he was soon elected to the provincial assembly, where he was noted more for his sophistication, aristocratic bearing, and aloof-

View of the naval stores industry in North Carolina

ness than for the radicalism he seemed to display in his call for an assembly independent of Governor Martin.

During the deliberations in Philadelphia the young lawyer took a leading part in the debates and established his reputation as an orator. John Adams spoke of him in the same breath with Richard Henry Lee and Patrick Henry, calling this trio the orators of the First Congress. Silas Deane of Connecticut lauded Hooper as "ingenius, polite, spirited, and tolerably eloquent." He impressed Benjamin Rush, the Philadelphia physician and delegate from Pennsylvania, as "a sensible, sprightly young lawyer, and a rapid, but correct speaker."

And Hooper's rhetoric brought results, for the forthright stand he took in the First Continental Congress for the nonexportation of American goods to England as well as the nonimportation of British goods undoubtedly influenced Congress's decision to apply economic sanctions as a means of bringing about changes in Britain's colonial policies. His support of sanctions was particularly courageous in view of North Carolina's thriving export trade in naval stores. Largely because of William Hooper, North Carolina left its mark on the first two Continental Congresses.

Joseph Hewes, the third delegate, differed markedly from Hooper in the way he represented North Carolina. While the latter made an impression with his oratory, the former remained virtually silent during the debates, but was "very useful upon committees." Hewes, though clearly an able man, might have owed his elections to Congress primarily to his popularity. Because of Hewes's pleasant personality, James Iredell, a prominent North Carolina leader, called him "one of the best and most agreeable men in the world." Coming from a New Jersey Quaker background and an apprenticeship under a Philadelphia merchant, Hewes had arrived in Edenton, North Carolina, by 1755. He had become one of Edenton's most prosperous merchants, acquiring vessels that conducted an extensive trade with Europe and the West Indies. Since 1766 he had represented the borough of Edenton in the provincial assembly.

Near the end of April, 1775, Hooper, Hewes, and Caswell made their second journey to Philadelphia. Hooper sailed aboard the schooner *Polly* from Wilmington, which then had a cosmopolitan population of approximately eight hundred and was considered by some to be "the most flourishing town in the province." In addition to its merchants, carpenters, mariners, and innkeepers, this thriving port town had twenty-four physicians!

Hewes and Caswell traveled north on horseback. On April 29

they left Halifax, a small town of about forty-five dwellings and perhaps two hundred people, which was located strategically on the trading paths between Virginia and South Carolina. Arriving at Port Tobacco, Maryland, on May 2, the two men joined Virginia's five delegates. All along the way the North Carolina and Virginia congressmen were honored by militia companies and local officials. The congressional caravan grew larger on May 8, when the seven men entered Wilmington, Delaware, and were joined there by delegates from Maryland and Delaware. The large group of congressmen was greeted, some six miles outside Philadelphia, by over five hundred men. Then "a company of riflemen and infantry, with a band of music" came out to escort them into the city. This enthusiastic display on May 9, climaxing a journey of eleven days for the North Carolinians, must have made even Caswell glad—at least for the moment—that he had been elected to an office which so many people respected. Upon reaching the city the two North Carolina delegates found that Hooper had been there since April 26.

Philadelphia in 1775 had around fifty-five hundred houses and a population variously estimated at between twenty-two thousand and thirty-five thousand. In addition to being the largest

Philadelphia, as it looked "from the Jersey Shore," published in 1768

city in America, it was one of the most hospitable—at least according to that famous Massachusetts delegate and future President, John Adams. His diary tells of endless rounds of dinners and banquets at which numerous delicacies and the best imported wines were served. There were "mighty feasts" and "sinful feasts," and some of the delegates became "very high." Between meals there was punch to drink and dried smoked sprats to eat. Entertainment abounded as the delegates were toasted and cheered. Strangely enough, some members of Congress shunned the parties—some because of preoccupation with the serious business to be conducted, some because of shyness, and others no doubt because such frolicking offended their moral sense. There were probably more such diversions during the early months of the struggle with England, but evidence suggests that parties continued sporadically all during the war.

In spite of the active social life available to those who wanted it, most of the North Carolina delegates did not like living in Philadelphia. Hooper, Hewes, and Caswell were all troubled by illness, Hooper suffering "frequent attacks of the Fever and Ague." He also complained constantly about the heat in summer and his poor accommodations. Exactly where the delegates lived

is not clear. They could have lodged at any of the twenty-five or thirty public houses on Second Street or at the seventeen or so higher class houses on High Street. According to John Adams, Joseph Hewes lived on Third Street. Some of the delegates took their meals from time to time at the City Tavern on Second Street, and, since that establishment also had several "elegant bed rooms, detached from noise, and as private as a lodging house," it is possible that some of North Carolina's congressmen roomed there.

Although living far from home caused discontent, the main reason for the North Carolina delegates' disenchantment with congressional service was what went on at the State House*—the drudgery of endless deliberations, the continuous committee work, and the news of glowing military successes followed by reports of debilitating disasters, all became the congressman's daily lot.

On May 10 when the three North Carolinians took their seats in the Second Congress, they could not know that the work of Congress would last for six years, until 1781. To handle the many matters that were before it, Congress appointed committees to reach decisions on specific questions and to make recommendations to the whole body. When the same questions kept coming up over and over—questions about money, ships, foreign affairs— Congress gradually established a number of standing committees, which eventually became administrative boards. For example, the Treasury Board dealt with financial matters, the Marine Board with ships (mostly naval vessels), and the Secret Committee (which did not use the word "board" but, in effect, was one) supervised trade. By 1781 there were at least eleven

---

* Unlike the First Continental Congress, which met at Carpenter's Hall, the Second Congress held its sessions in the State House, later to be renamed Independence Hall. Most of the men who attended the First Congress were reelected to attend the Second, although there were a few new faces. The number of delegates constantly fluctuated during the Second Congress.

Birch Print, 2nd Street. North from Market Street, with Christ Church, Philadelphia

standing boards. This arrangement changed under the Confederation Congress, when executive departments replaced standing boards. The use of committees, however, continued.

Early in the Second Continental Congress Hooper was appointed chairman of two committees. One committee drafted an explanation to Jamaica of why the mainland colonies had decided to stop trading with the West Indies. The other drafted a resolution urging that July 20 be set aside as "a day of humiliation, fasting, and prayer. . . ." Hewes received several important committee assignments that summer. One was to a finance committee, which was responsible for estimating the amount of money needed for defense in the event of war with England. His second committee drafted rules and regulations for an army, if one should be required, and his third committee inquired into the lead and ore resources of the colonies. Unlike his fellow North Carolinians, Caswell received no assignment of significance. He was put on only one committee to confer with Charles Lee about becoming an officer in the Continental Army.

The daily routine of the North Carolina delegates was taxing for those who received committee and board assignments. They sat in Congress from nine in the morning until six in the evening and attended committee meetings at night. Joseph Hewes had been at work only a few months in 1775 when he declared that he was "weary of politics." By autumn additional committee assignments and an appointment to the demanding Naval (later Marine) Board were enough to make him cast longing eyes toward North Carolina, but he remained at his post, and his assignments increased the next year.

Part of the duty of every North Carolina delegate was "to advise, confer, debate, resolve and determine for and in behalf of" North Carolina all questions raised in Congress. Most of the North Carolinians who would attend Congress during the war years were not orators, and were therefore reluctant to engage in the debates. One exception, of course, was Hooper.

On August 1, after three weary months in Philadelphia, the Second Continental Congress adjourned, agreeing to reassemble on September 5. Hooper, who had once again been ill and had suffered from the intense summer heat, soon sailed for North Carolina. Apparently Hewes had departed some days before the adjournment. He had also endured bad health, particularly trouble with his eyes. He informed his friend James Iredell that it caused him pain to write and that he could "scarcely see to read" what he had written.

But there was little respite for the congressional delegates in North Carolina. Hooper, Hewes, and Caswell were all delegates to the Third Provincial Congress, which convened in Hillsborough on August 20, and they played important parts in the proceedings. That assembly created a provisional government for the province, initiated plans for raising a large number of troops, and reelected the three men who had served North Carolina in the Continental Congress from its inception. Caswell, however, was named on September 8 as treasurer for the Southern District of North Carolina and resigned his seat in the Continental Congress. To replace him the provincial congress chose John Penn.

Like Hooper, Hewes, and Caswell, Penn was not a native North Carolinian, having been born in Caroline County, Virginia, in 1741. Unlike the others, he was not a tidewater aristocrat. He had studied law with Edmund Pendleton in Virginia and, after having practiced for twelve years in his native county, had moved in 1774 to Granville County, which was then the North Carolina backcountry. Penn's election to the Continental Congress was significant politically, for it indicated that the age-old bitterness between the hinterland and the tidewater was not dead. Backcountry farmers had consistently accused eastern, aristocratic political leaders of ignoring western interests. In the late 1760s and early 1770s the westerners had launched the Regulator Movement to protest corruption among their local officials, who were appointed by the royal governor. But the Regulators had been defeated by forces of Governor William Tryon in 1771. Hooper, Hewes, and Caswell had all stood with the governor against the Regulators. When these three delegates subsequently called for resistance against England and held positions of leadership, westerners were reluctant to endorse their cause or to fight alongside their longtime enemies. But by the time the Third Provincial Congress met, the hinterlanders *were* involved and demanded a voice in determining the course of action against Great Britain. Thus the old east-west sectional controversy sent its ripples through the Third Congress. To prevent cleavage in the American resistance movement, the North Carolina congress chose Penn, who was presumably sympathetic to democratic ideals rather than to tidewater Whig elitism.

Although the Continental Congress was supposed to reconvene on September 5, the North Carolina delegates did not reach Philadelphia until the following month—Penn on October 12, and his two colleagues on October 22. Harmony had always prevailed among the North Carolina delegates, but now Hooper and Hewes chose to remain aloof from Penn. The last few months of 1775 were busy ones for Hooper and Hewes, both of whom had received important committee assignments. But Penn was ignored by Congress. One political issue appeared—small that autumn but soon to be large—and showed that Penn saw things a little differently from Hooper and Hewes. The latter two vigorously supported a movement to make Transylvania (now Kentucky) the fourteenth colony. North Carolina merchant James Hogg was sent to Philadelphia to represent the interests of the would-be colony and was judiciously introduced by Hooper and Hewes to several members of Congress. These two delegates also gave to various congressmen a "favorable account" of the plan of the Transylvania proprietors (mostly land speculators

John Penn

from tidewater North Carolina) to make their western settlements one of the colonies. Other matters were more pressing at
the time Hogg appeared in Philadelphia to lobby for the Transylvania Company, and Congress did not seriously consider
making a colony of the company's western settlements at that
time. The question of the land beyond the mountains was, however, to come up again and keep Congress occupied for years to
come. For the moment Penn avoided the political issue of western
lands, perhaps because Transylvania was a project sponsored
largely by tidewater promoters, or possibly because he had no
personal, vested interest in the venture. Although it cannot be
stated with certainty why Penn did not speak up on the issue
of western expansion in the fall of 1775, it can be demonstrated

from his service in Congress after 1775 that he frequently disagreed with his colleagues from the coastal plains on political questions. North Carolina's delegation in Congress would never experience the disharmony that plagued some of the other delegations, but the acrimony which had long prevailed in North Carolina's east-west relations would continue to arise from time to time.

There is also some evidence that Penn's social life interfered with his congressional duties. He showered much attention upon the young women of the famous Shippen family, enjoyed the night life in Philadelphia, and apparently fought at least one duel. While the other members of the North Carolina delegation were working day and night, Penn spent much time socializing. His colleagues seem to have thought that Congress was ignoring Penn and not the other way around, for their comments on his outside activities were more humorous than resentful. However, they *were* occasionally annoyed by Penn's lightheartedness and probably thought that Congress would have given him more to do if he had been available more often.

As 1775 ended and the days of 1776 began to follow one upon another, Congress came face to face with its most important decision. The First Congress had decided to impose economic sanctions against British trade to secure redress of grievances and reconciliation. Now, because of an increasing ground swell throughout the colonies for political separation from the mother country, Congress had to decide whether to cling to its original objective or to change it to a new one—independence. Hooper, Hewes, and Penn, forced to resolve this hard question in the early months of 1776, went through some intense inner struggles.

2

from resistance to revolution: 1774-1776

CONTROVERSY BETWEEN Great Britain and its American colonies had entered a new and critically dangerous phase in 1774, but this was not immediately apparent to the men North Carolina sent to Congress. To them it was the same old family quarrel. Hooper, Hewes, Caswell, and Penn went to Philadelphia to prevent a revolution, not to start one.

"Look to the reigning monarch of Britain as your rightful and lawful Sovereign[;] dare every danger & difficulty in support of his person[,] Crown & dignity," the delegates admonished the people of North Carolina in June, 1775. Hewes called George III a "most gracious Sovereign" and vowed that he and his colleagues would sacrifice their lives for him. The North Carolina congressmen had no desire to disavow the British Constitution because they revered the British concept of government. Nor did they wish to depose George III or secede from the British Empire. They merely wanted His Majesty to dismiss his ministers, whom they regarded as "enemies to the freedom of the human race."

Even so, the delegates' allegiance to the British crown had limits. King George, they insisted, must uphold the liberties guaranteed to all his subjects, including Americans, by the British Constitution. British policies which threatened those liberties would have to be altered. If they were not, then the time might come when the American objective would change from redress of grievances to independence. As early as July, 1775, Hewes wrote that "every American to a man" would "die or be free."

Hooper's attitude was essentially the same. He expressed "a Sincere love for the Constitution of G. Britain," but he feared that no concessions would be won from Lord North, the king's chief minister, except those "purchased at the point of the Sword." Yet, at the same time, Hooper spoke approvingly of George III.

The North Carolina delegates, in taking a firm position in favor of reconciliation, reflected the sentiment of their constituents. The Third Provincial Congress voted approval of the way Hooper, Hewes, and Caswell had represented North Carolina in Philadelphia, but to insure that they would not be attracted to independence, the congress instructed them to reject any plan of union among the colonies without first securing the approval of the provincial congress. The provincial congress feared that the formation of a union would be a positive step toward independence.

Even though the American objective still professed to be reconciliation, fighting had erupted in Massachusetts and Canada. The Second Continental Congress, therefore, exerted every effort to strengthen American defenses. In this task they looked more to Hooper than to the other North Carolina delegates, primarily because Hooper had clearly demonstrated his leadership abilities during the First Continental Congress.

As Hooper, Hewes, and Penn performed their duties in Congress they did not veer, in the closing months of 1775, from the course of reconciliation. Hooper demonstrated his reluctance to support any action that the British government might interpret as a move toward independence when he served on the committee to consider the problem of South Carolina. The committee report recommended that South Carolina be assured that Congress would accept any government which that province might form. Hooper objected to the report. To him it repudiated reconciliation, since South Carolina's new provincial government would be formed independently of the mother country. Hooper's objections were brushed aside, however, and Congress adopted the report on November 4.

As the end of 1775 approached, Hooper and his two colleagues began to despair of reconciliation. Hooper and Hewes were especially apprehensive because they began to see signs of genuine political and social revolution looming on the horizon. Such an eventuality might easily result, they concluded, in the erosion of their influence in provincial politics. Had they not just five years earlier sided with the established order to help crush the Regulators? Common people like most of the Regulators would almost certainly expect—indeed demand—participation if a completely new provincial government had to be formed. Hooper and Hewes, no friends of democracy, did not want this. There also remained their long-standing respect and admiration for the mother country. As late as January 6, 1776, Hooper called upon "heaven" to check the "approaching ruin" of Great Britain and make her once again "the guardian of freedom."

Unlike Hooper and Hewes, Penn had no established place to lose in North Carolina politics. This might lead one to assume that Penn was in the vanguard of the independence movement. Actually he was not. While he did not pale before the spectre of separation, neither did he welcome the prospect of leaving the British Empire. Primarily concerned about commercial and monetary problems that might follow independence, he continued to favor pressuring Great Britain into guaranteeing American liberties. This was his position as late as February, 1776.

Through January and February of the new year the three delegates, then, clung to the last thread of hope that secession could be avoided. By March, however, they were convinced that the thread had snapped and separation was inevitable. Hooper ceased praising George III and condemned him as a haughty monarch; Hewes saw "no prospect of a reconciliation" and "nothing left to do but fight it out"; and Penn proposed that the colonies make foreign alliances, the certain prelude to an irrevocable split with the mother country.

The main factor in the delegates' acceptance of the idea of independence was Great Britain's uncompromising attitude. The king's August 23 proclamation declaring the colonies to be in rebellion and the December 22 proclamation closing all American ports to trade as of March 1, 1776, reached Congress early in 1776 and were interpreted by the North Carolina delegates—especially Penn—as a British attempt to bind Americans with the chains of slavery. The delegates were also distressed by reports that the king had hired a large number of German mercenaries to fight in America.

An event which occurred in North Carolina on February 27, 1776, pushed Hooper, Hewes, and Penn further down the road to independence. This was the Battle of Moore's Creek Bridge, fought between North Carolinians who were loyal to the crown and those who were Patriots. The Loyalist force, commanded by General Donald McDonald, suffered a serious defeat at the hands of the Patriots, who were ably led by former Continental delegate Richard Caswell and Alexander Lillington. Now that blood had been spilled in North Carolina, the people of the province and their delegates in Congress, too, began to consider more seriously the merits of independence.

Although the congressional delegates sensed that public opinion was changing in North Carolina, they wanted definite instructions before championing the cause of independence. They urged Samuel Johnston, who had assumed a central place of leadership in North Carolina politics, to sound out the sentiment of

Battle at Moore's Creek Bridge

Constitution House in Halifax, North Carolina, a meeting place of the General Assembly

the province at the Fourth Provincial Congress, soon to meet in Halifax. If North Carolina really wanted independence, its three delegates in the Continental Congress were prepared to support a movement for it.

After giving the matter more thought, the delegates must have concluded that they should express their views in person at the Fourth Congress, for Hooper and Penn hurried off to attend it. The trip to Halifax took eighteen days, and Hooper pictured the arduous journey as "fatiguing beyond all description." Upon arrival, Hooper and Penn discovered that the provincial congress had already taken a step toward independence. The famous Hali-

And Whereas the Moderation hitherto manifested by the united Colonies, and their sincere desire to reconciled to the Mother Country on Constitutional principles, have procured no Mitigation of the aforesaid Wrongs and Usurpations, and no hopes remain of obtaining redress, by those means alone which have been hitherto tried, Your Committee are of Opinion that the House should enter into the following Resolve,

Resolved that the Delegates for this Colony in the Continental Congress be impowered to Concur with the Delegates of the other Colonies in declaring Independency and forming foreign Alliances — reserving to this Colony, the Sole and Exclusive right of forming a Constitution and Laws for this Colony, and of appointing Delegates from time to time under the direction of a General Representation thereof, to meet the Delegates of the other Colonies for such purposes as shall be hereafter pointed out.

The Congress taking the same into Consideration Unanimously Concurred therewith

By order
Jas. Green jun secy

The Halifax Resolves,
April 12, 1776

fax Resolves of April 12 empowered North Carolina's delegates in the Continental Congress "to concur with the delegates of the other Colonies in declaring Independency, and forming foreign alliances. . . ." Penn, obviously excited about the decision of the Fourth Provincial Congress, soon wrote John Adams that here "all regard and fondness for the King or the nation of Great Britain" were gone and that what North Carolinians wanted was "total separation." "Independence," he went on to remark, "is the word most used. . . ." Undoubtedly the Granville County lawyer took pride in the action of the Fourth Provincial Congress, for North Carolina, by making the first formal provincial endorsement of separation, had become the leader of the American colonies in plunging into the unfathomed waters of independence.

Meanwhile, in Philadelphia, Hewes sat as North Carolina's only congressional delegate. Late in April he received a copy of the Halifax Resolves. Apparently because he did not want to act alone in encouraging a movement for independence, Hewes delayed presenting the Resolves to Congress for a whole month.* But—at last—on May 27, the same day that Virginia's delegates presented even stronger resolutions from their province, Hewes laid the Halifax Resolves before Congress. Eleven days later Richard Henry Lee proposed his momentous resolution for independence, consideration of which, after two days of debate, was postponed until July 1.

Penn, who returned to Philadelphia about June 20, joined

---

* The musical play and movie, "1776," leave the impression that Hewes fell under the domination of the South Carolina delegates during the spring of 1776 when he sat alone for North Carolina in Congress. Actually this is misleading, but such a conclusion is understandable. Hewes was a shy man in public and, being a most congenial fellow, appeared to go along with whomever he accompanied. Behind the scenes he was much more forceful. During the period in question he served on numerous congressional committees and four standing boards, taking a leading part in the activities of the important Marine Board.

Hewes in a prediction that independence would supersede reconciliation as the main American objective by early July. Hewes wrote James Iredell, his close friend and political ally, that he expected Congress to vote for independence by "a great majority" and that Americans would take for themselves "a new name." Penn said that the decision soon to be made would be for *total* separation.

The two North Carolina delegates had measured the sentiment of Congress accurately, for on July 2 the representatives of twelve colonies—those from New York abstaining—resolved "that these United Colonies are and of Right ought to be, Free and Independent States. . . ." Debate on Thomas Jefferson's formal Declaration of Independence followed on July 3, and, after making some minor changes, Congress approved the famous document on July 4. Not until August 2, however, was the Declaration signed, thus enabling William Hooper, who had returned to Philadelphia on July 23, to join the other members of Congress in signing it.

What many had long feared—a war for independence—had come. The resistance movement which North Carolina's delegates had helped to launch had turned into a full-fledged political revolution. Although not in the forefront of the effort to set a course toward separation, the North Carolina delegates had endorsed independence when their constituents embraced it. And yet, all three of the North Carolinians, especially Hooper, had reservations about the formation of an independent government. They feared that such a government might incorporate more elements of broad, popular representation than were compatible with their conservative, Whig beliefs. After gauging the sentiment of the Fourth Provincial Congress, Hooper had warned Hewes in a letter not to "hint" about any possibility of "future reconciliation" unless he wanted to be accused of "Toryism." Hooper suggested that they "Swim on the democratick flood," for any attempt to check it would result in their being "buried in it." Besides, the tidewater lawyer had become convinced that enough "misery" had been heaped upon Americans by Great Britain and that separation could not be worse than the existing situation. Hewes and Penn, like Hooper, were torn between their admiration and affection for the mother country and their devotion to American rights, which all three genuinely believed were being denied by unconstitutional and ill-advised British policies.

Once American resistance against Great Britain became a struggle for independence, North Carolina's representatives in Congress worked diligently to ensure that the Continental Congress furnish the necessary supplies to their state. In 1776 Hooper, Hewes, and Penn arranged to have wagons loaded with gunpowder, arms, salt pans, and military guides sent to North Carolina. One shipment in August included 144 sets of Simes's military guides,* twenty-four books about military discipline, and some copies of the Reverend John Witherspoon's sermons. Witherspoon, a Presbyterian minister and president of Princeton College, was known for his persuasive sermons which demonstrated, conclusively to many, that God and America were on the same side. The North Carolina delegates probably hoped Witherspoon's sermons would have a salutary influence on North Carolina's backcountry Presbyterians, who, they had heard, were slow to support the American cause. Actually they worried needlessly, because the Presbyterians, after only a brief hesitation, had already embraced the cause of independence.

In the spring of 1776 Hewes had feared that separation from Great Britain would bring financial chaos to America. After the

---

* Thomas Simes, *The Military Guide for Young Officers*, 2 volumes, published in London and Philadelphia, 1776. Volume II was entitled *A New Military, Historical, and Explanatory Dictionary: Including the Warriors Gazetteer of Places Remarkable for Sieges or Battles*. These guides purported to give one "a competent knowledge of the art" of warfare.

issue was decided, however, Hewes discovered that a long war could provide a businessman with many opportunities for making money. The Revolutionary War was good to Hewes, but he did much more than take care of his financial interests—he served the American cause with a great deal of dedication. Though his health was failing in the summer of 1776, he remained in Congress until late September. During that period he desperately attempted to lighten his load, but as a member of the highly important Marine, Secret, and Treasury boards, he found relief to be elusive. The duties connected with these boards involved making decisions on matters that Hewes as a merchant knew best—ships, supplies, and money. His membership on the Secret Committee made business opportunities available to him. When he left Philadelphia in the early autumn of 1776 for a rest in Edenton, he went as a commissioned agent of the Secret Committee. Apparently he secured a similar commission for his business partner, Robert Smith, for they were soon doing the committee's business together. They were empowered to issue contracts for the construction and fitting out of naval vessels, to import and export naval supplies, to distribute prize money when enemy ships were seized, and to account to Congress quarterly for all funds expended. Having this inside track, Hewes easily arranged the rental of his own ships to Congress.

While Hewes was slowly making a fortune, Penn, the first North Carolina delegate to come out forthrightly for independence, was struggling to keep his seat in Congress. The Fifth Provincial Congress, which met in Halifax during November and December, 1776, unseated Penn in favor of Thomas Burke, a rising star in state politics. But in April, 1777, when North Carolina's first General Assembly, formed under the new state constitution of 1776, met at New Bern, Penn maneuvered himself into Hewes's congressional seat. Penn charged that Hewes had delayed his return to Congress in the spring of 1777 because he was making so much money as an agent for the Secret Committee. Furthermore, Penn argued, the fact that Hewes was a delegate to Congress *and* an agent of the Secret Committee meant that he was holding two important offices simultaneously—a clear violation of the new state constitution. So persuasive was Penn that the Assembly chose him to serve with Hooper and Burke, and ousted Hewes. Thus Penn went back to Congress, but the quality of his service did not improve. There is no evidence that experience made Penn a better legislator. From time to time he would make minor contributions in debates, but his overall record was mediocre at best.

Of the three North Carolina delegates who signed the Declaration of Independence, Hooper alone had serious difficulty adjusting to the spirit of that document. Penn could discern in the Revolution a chance to enhance his political fortune, and Hewes could accept it as a business opportunity. Hooper, however, was a man incapable of easily abandoning deep-seated principles. Immediately after the decision for independence, no one was more dedicated to the new cause than Hooper, and few in Congress worked harder than he during the closing months of 1776 when he alone represented North Carolina. Hewes was in Edenton. Near the end of October, Penn left Philadelphia to attend the Fifth Provincial Congress. Hooper was left to carry his state's burden in the Continental Congress. His record for that trying period clearly indicates that he did his duty with diligence and devotion. He served on fourteen committees and five standing boards. As a member of the War, Treasury, Marine, and State-of-Prisoners boards and the Committee of Secret Correspondence, he helped make decisions of the utmost importance with regard to conducting and financing the war and seeking foreign alliances.

Although Hooper labored indefatigably in Congress toward the end of 1776, he was not the Hooper of earlier days. The fires

Home of Joseph Hewes in Edenton, North Carolina

of his enthusiasm burned lower and lower, for he could see that America and North Carolina were taking the political turn toward popular government which he had foreseen and dreaded. He was further discouraged by George Washington's defeat in New York and his retreat across New Jersey. Hooper blamed the reverses on the lethargy of Pennsylvania, which had ignored Washington's plea for militia assistance. In December, Hooper disgustedly wrote, "We do not deserve to be saved."

Everything seemed to turn sour, not only in Congress but back home in North Carolina. In September and October, before the Fifth Provincial Congress met at Halifax on November 12 to draft a state constitution, Hooper had let it be known through several letters that he favored an instrument of government based on the British Constitution, which he claimed was as nearly perfect as any could be "within the compass of human abilities." He cautioned against a "motley mixture of limited monarchy and an execrable democracy—a Beast without a head." In other words, he thought it essential to have a strong executive and to avoid an all-powerful unicameral legislature, which, though he did not say so forthrightly, would presumably be a popularly elected body. Since the Fifth Congress was divided fairly equally between advocates of popular government and supporters of elitist rule, some kind of compromise was inevitable. Consequently neither side was happy with the resulting constitution, an instrument which gave North Carolina a bicameral legislature and an executive with severely limited powers. This was hardly what Hooper wanted.

The Wilmington lawyer suffered more disappointment upon learning that in his own home county his election to the Fifth Provincial Congress had been bitterly contested. Believing that his past service entitled him to "unanimous reappointment" by his "Country," he decided that he did not desire "further fatigue." In January, 1777, he waited to be joined by his old friend Hewes

Home of William Hooper

and the newly-elected Thomas Burke in Baltimore, where Congress, fearing a British attack on Philadelphia, had fled. He especially disliked Baltimore, which he called a "dirty, boggy hole," the "worst of all possible places." During those anxious days, Hooper probably decided to give up his seat in Congress.

If there was any hope that Hooper might change his mind about returning to Congress, it went up in the smoke of the political battles at the meeting of the first General Assembly in April. Penn's election to Congress in place of Hewes, plus the fact that Burke had received twice as many votes as Hooper, prompted the latter to resign his congressional seat. Attempting to bow out gracefully, Hooper said that "the Claims of social & Domestic life & the situation" of his "private affairs" would no longer "suffer" him to "engage in a publick Service." The true reason for Hooper's withdrawal was that, in his eyes, North Carolina had sealed its ingratitude for his service by the action of the General Assembly at New Bern. Also, he could plainly see that his once-great influence was waning.

Hooper's retirement from public life did not last long. He soon won election to the General Assembly and held a seat for the next six years. In 1784 he was elected again, this time serving only one term. Meanwhile, he had experienced personal misfortune. During the British occupation of Wilmington in 1781 he had had to flee from his home into the interior and for a while remained separated from his family. When this bitter experience was over, he moved from Wilmington to Hillsborough. There he established his reputation as one of North Carolina's leading lawyers. At the time of the controversy over the adoption of the new Federal Constitution in 1788, Hooper fought for ratification—figuratively and literally, for an angered antifederalist blackened both his eyes. No doubt Hooper was pleased to see North Carolina finally join the new union a little less than a year before he died on October 14, 1790, at age forty-eight.

William Hooper, Joseph Hewes, and John Penn had one outstanding thing in common—the moment of glory they shared as North Carolina's signers of the Declaration of Independence. That glory soon faded. Hewes died more than four years before the war ended. Penn was replaced in Congress and later made worthy contributions as a member of the North Carolina Board of War, but by 1783 he was out of the political limelight. Hooper and his conservative friends were far removed from popular favor—at least for the time being. The Revolution had given the three men fame and, almost as quickly, had taken it away.

North Carolina signers of the Declaration of Independence

Thomas Burke

3

the confederation: 1777

THOMAS BURKE arrived in Baltimore and joined William Hooper on February 1, 1777. Four days later Hooper, just recovering from a serious illness, departed for home on horseback. His service in the Continental Congress was over forever. The man who had come to relieve Hooper was destined to gain even greater distinction as a legislator. For over four years North Carolina would be represented in Congress by its most outstanding delegate.

Born in Ireland, Burke came to America in 1763, after a quarrel with his family. Though only a teen-ager (if 1747, the year usually given for his birth, is accurate), he established a medical practice in Accomac County, Virginia, but he soon left medicine for the law and opened a practice in Norfolk. In 1772 he moved to Hillsborough in the North Carolina backcountry, and there, though continuing his legal practice, he became a country gentleman on his estate, Tyaquin, a mile or two north of town. The political crises of 1774 and 1775 gave Burke, who had written popular poetry against the Stamp Act in 1765, another opportunity to oppose Great Britain. Now a lawyer in his late twenties instead of a teen-aged poet, Burke became influential politically. He made his presence felt as a member of the North Carolina provincial congresses, and when the fifth congress met at Halifax in November, 1776, he helped write North Carolina's new state constitution.

With only one good eye and a face marked by smallpox, Burke was far from impressive-looking, but he was brilliant. Though merry, congenial, and witty most of the time, he could also be rude, opinionated, and obstinate. Tact was one thing of which he had little. He showed no reluctance to participate—immediately and emphatically—in the proceedings of the Continental Congress. He had hardly arrived when he cut a path through that body like a comet across the sky. His new colleagues recognized his talents; but they also noted his arrogance, his dogmatism, his vanity, and his air of superiority. Quick to take offense and always argumentative, Burke lost no time in making a host of enemies.

No one would have guessed in the early months of 1777 that Burke was headed for greatness, as he seemed to take the negative side of every issue, basing his arguments more often on emotion than on logic. His arrival in Congress coincided with the beginning of several months of debate on the question of a formal political union between the thirteen struggling states. Should the states enter into a union, and, if so, what kind of union should it be? Burke had strong feelings about these questions, and he showed no hesitation in expressing them. To this versatile and volatile Irishman the vital issue in forming a union was the danger that the states might surrender their powers to any central government which might be formed, and he immediately and forthrightly declared in favor of sovereignty for each state. At this stage of his political development Burke stood firmly for cooperation between the states, but not for union, and especially not for a union that would give a central government any measure of power. If there had to be a union or confederation, at all, it should not, Burke contended, be established until the war was won. Those who opposed Burke's views (including Cornelius Harnett, who joined Burke as a member of the North Carolina delegation later in 1777) took the position that no foreign alliances could be made before a union was formed, and without alliances the American states might well lose the war. In other words, union was necessary to help assure survival.

The question of power weighed so heavily on Burke's mind, however, that no one could persuade him to look at the positive side of forming a confederation. Fearing that Congress might eventually emulate the bad example of Parliament in misusing power, Burke wanted severe limitations placed on Congressional authority—in the event that the sentiment for union could not be repressed. Men, Burke believed, had a strong urge to exercise control over other men, an urge stemming from "the Delusive Intoxication which power naturally imposes on the human mind."

With his fear that power would slip away from the states, Burke struggled vigorously against any action by Congress, the existing *de facto* central government, that might increase the authority of that body at the expense of the states' authority. For example, Congress, during February of 1777, empowered special individuals to arrest deserters from the Continental Army without consulting the governments of their home states. Burke insisted that such peremptory seizures of alleged deserters would set a bad precedent, because an innocent citizen might be taken arbitrarily and imprisoned without the opportunity to claim the legal protection guaranteed to him by his own state government. The North Carolina delegate demanded that his dissent be recorded in the Congressional Journals and, through his protest, succeeded in having the matter reconsidered. In the lengthy debate that followed, Burke was forced to confront such worthies as James Wilson, John Adams, and Richard Henry Lee. Wilson, an able Pennsylvania delegate, argued that the regulation of the army was a responsibility of the Continental Congress and urged Congress to stand up for its right to apprehend deserters.

The outspoken Burke did not agree. He contended that the

home states of deserters should have jurisdiction over them and that Congress had no right to usurp that power. Burke abhorred Wilson's willingness to permit the army to disregard the laws of the states and attempted to coax from him a retraction of his position. Repeatedly arguing that only the states could "act coercively against their Citizens," Burke finally inflated the issue out of all proportion. He went so far as to claim that giving Congress this right would be equal to giving that body unlimited power "over the Lives and Liberties of all men in America." Burke's impassioned rhetoric, at least in this instance, was no match for the common-sense arguments of Wilson and those who stood with him. The original resolution to give Congress control over Continental Army deserters remained unaltered.

During the same month, February, 1777, in which the debate over deserters occurred, Burke and Wilson again crossed swords over the question of who had what power. When the Pennsylvanian came out in favor of a motion allowing Congress to approve or reject actions taken by individual states, Burke, as could be expected, took the opposite position. Declaring that he had no intention of relinquishing the rights of his state, Burke maintained that North Carolina could take any action it pleased— with or without the approval of Congress. After all, he implied, Congress was nothing more than a body of diplomatic representatives from the thirteen sovereign states.

Burke was almost paranoid in his attitude concerning North Carolina's sovereignty. He took every opportunity to assert his position, and occasionally he cleverly stretched a point at issue to create such an opportunity. In late February, when some members of Congress proposed that the body return to Philadalphia from Baltimore, Burke and all the southern delegates except those from Georgia stood against it. Contending that Congress should not interrupt the important business before it, the North Carolinian moved to delay the question. He based his action on the belief that any one state had the privilege of postponing a vote. John Adams, James Wilson, and Roger Sherman disagreed strongly with Burke. They argued that a majority vote was necessary to determine whether a state "should be permitted to exercise the right of postponing the Question." Burke stood his ground, insisting that a procedural rule previously agreed upon by common consent could not be abrogated by a mere majority vote of Congress. Moreover, he warned that putting the question to a vote would represent a serious enough invasion of the rights of North Carolina to prompt the state to withdraw from Congress. This time Burke had substantial support, and the question was not put to a vote.

Whatever satisfaction Burke gained from arguing his opponents down on this question was short-lived. For Congress ended its sojourn in Baltimore on February 27. The members agreed to reassemble in Philadelphia on March 4, but there was not a sufficient number of delegates for a quorum until March 12. Thus it was that in April, 1777, Philadelphia was the battlefield upon which Burke won his greatest victory for state sovereignty. When the amended draft of John Dickinson's Articles of Confederation was discussed, Burke contended that Article III gave the supreme power of the new government to Congress and not to the states. The only power reserved to the states, Burke argued, was control of their internal security. To prevent future Congresses from accumulating unlimited power, the North Carolina delegate proposed an amendment by which the states would retain their sovereignty, freedom, and independence, as well as all powers that were not expressly delegated to Congress. Burke's proposal carried and was incorporated as Article II of the Articles of Confederation—and became a millstone around the Confederation's neck following ratification of the Articles in 1781. The fiery Irishman had made certain that America—as long as the Articles of Confederation remained its constitution—would be a land of thirteen separate states.

There were more debates on the Confederation in May and

June, and during that time Burke reached the conclusion that the states would never be able to resolve their differences and agree upon a plan of government. The major difficulty in union, he decided, was the problem of giving each state its "proper weight in the public Council. . . ." Put another way, the states would never agree on a method for determining the voting power that each would have in the national legislature. Although convinced that the states would ultimately come to terms on nothing stronger than a defensive alliance, Burke attempted to bring the large and small states together by offering a compromise solution. He proposed, in an amendment to the Articles, a two-house legislature. His plan included a General Council to be chosen by the states and a Council of State to consist of one delegate from each state, also to be chosen by the states. Undoubtedly Burke was trying to erect safeguards against an all-powerful legislature. If there were two houses, each could prevent the other from acquiring too much power. The proposal gained little support, and Congress voted it down.

As debates over the Confederation continued, Burke, drained physically by being North Carolina's lone representative in Congress for four months, eagerly awaited the arrival of someone to assist him. In early June news reached him that he would soon be joined by John Penn and Cornelius Harnett, after which he would be free to leave his duties for a visit with his family. And to make the news even better, Governor Richard Caswell informed the exhausted delegate that the General Assembly of North Carolina had named a county for him. This honor, an impressive tribute to Burke, no doubt increased his prestige in Congress.

On June 23 John Penn finally appeared in Congress. Reaching Philadelphia ahead of Penn, however, was a letter from Joseph Hewes which informed Burke of the tactics used by Penn at New Bern in April to win Hewes's Congressional seat. According to

The Sons of Liberty, led by Cornelius Harnett, preparing to turn away British ships carrying tax stamps

Hewes, Penn was "much Mortified" at the prospect of serving with Burke, fearing that there was "not a very good understanding" between them. Then, taking a verbal shot at Penn, Hewes implied that his successor's arrival in Philadelphia would not afford Burke much relief from work. The remarks of Hewes must not have prejudiced Burke against his new colleague, for the two men apparently worked together harmoniously.

Illness, bad weather, and an adverse reaction to a smallpox inoculation kept Cornelius Harnett, North Carolina's great man from the Lower Cape Fear, from joining Burke and Penn in Philadelphia until July 18. His reputation preceded him. A wealthy merchant and distiller of rum in Wilmington, he had won fame as the leader and one of the organizers of the Sons of Liberty, who, in 1766, had forcefully kept the royal governor from imposing the hated Stamp Act in the colony of North Carolina. In 1773 Josiah Quincy, Jr., of Massachusetts had visited Harnett in Wilmington and had lauded him as "the Sam Adams of North Carolina." The numerous disputes since 1774 between the colonies and the mother country had found Harnett once again vitally involved in the movement to resist British policies. His leadership in the state remained as staunch and effective as it had been in 1766.

By the time the wealthy Wilmington merchant was elected to Congress he was almost sixty years old and troubled by severe attacks of gout, which would put him in bed for days at a time. He probably would not be remembered at all for his role in Congress had he not taken such a forthright stand in favor of the Confederation, thereby providing a ponderous counterweight to Burke's determined opposition to union. Both Harnett and Burke had helped write the North Carolina constitution of 1776, and both men enjoyed great prestige. On the question of union, however, they viewed matters quite differently. This was significant, for without support for the Confederation from someone of enormous reputation like Harnett's, Burke would most likely have blocked the ratification of the Articles of Confederation in North Carolina. The stage was set for a gigantic struggle among North Carolina political leaders over the two opposing points of view articulated by Harnett and Burke on the issue of union.

What contribution Harnett would make in Congress was, of course, not known in the summer of 1777. But some members of that body, having heard of his past deeds and having been informed of his talents, looked forward to his participation. The distinguished Robert Morris of Pennsylvania made a special effort to welcome him. In May, William Hooper had written Morris to tell him that Harnett was "a judicious man, and a sensible, agreeable companion." Elaborating on Harnett's great wealth and knowledge of trade, Hooper assured Morris that Harnett would be useful "on some . . . Mercantile committees."

In July when Harnett arrived, North Carolina, for the first time since September of 1776, had three men in Congress at the

Home of Cornelius Harnett, torn down in 1904

same time. Generally Burke, Harnett, and Penn worked together without serious discord, but there were disagreements over minor matters and at least one major one. One minor point of dispute centered around correspondence. Harnett, who may have wanted to keep a close watch on Burke and Penn, or whose troubles with the gout may have dampened his enthusiasm for writing, wished to send all official reports jointly, but his two colleagues thought this unnecessary. On the major question of the Confederation, Harnett quickly found himself at odds with Burke's extreme position on the sovereignty of states. What Penn was thinking at this point about that issue is not clear. A pygmy at work between two giants, he was apparently not yet sure which one to offend.

Harnett had not been in Philadelphia long when the city was threatened by the advance of the British army. The danger had been imaginary when Congress had fled to Baltimore the previous December, but this time it was genuine. When Washington's army was all but smashed at Brandywine trying to stop the British on September 11, 1777, and the hard-pressed American troops fell back toward Philadelphia, the members of Congress again shook the dust of the beleaguered city from their shoes and retreated westward to York, a town of eighteen hundred inhabitants in the Pennsylvania backcountry. Congress assembled there on September 30, but Harnett was the only North Carolina delegate present. Penn did not arrive until October 3, and Burke, who had gone to observe the fighting at Brandywine, appeared a week later. Remaining for only a few days, Burke departed for North Carolina on October 14 for his long-awaited rest.

Soon after reaching York the Continental delegates began to discuss once more the matter of union. Penn, at last committing himself and following the lead of Harnett instead of Burke, expressed the view that some kind of confederation had to be formed or the new nation would perish in its infancy. On October 10 Harnett wrote to Governor Caswell assuring him that, if Congress agreed upon a plan of union, "Penn and myself will embrace the earliest opportunity of transmitting it to your Excellency." For about six weeks debate raged over the problems of representation, the basis of taxation, and the land west of the mountains which various states claimed.

During the deliberations Harnett and Penn, though not displaying Burke's extreme anxiety over state sovereignty, were not far behind the Irishman in their desire to protect the rights of the individual states. While they conceded that Congress might regulate trade by treaties, they also supported a provision that no treaty of commerce negotiated by Congress should interfere with the right of a state to levy "imposts and duties." Harnett and Penn also accepted the principle that the acts and judicial proceedings of a state should be honored by the other states, but they opposed an amendment which would allow a citizen of one state to recover a debt in a different state. On the question of western lands the two North Carolina delegates naturally sided with the states, which, like their state, claimed western lands. They voted against a recommendation by the small states which had no western land that each state that had such lands should furnish Congress a description of their claims, an enormously complicated process which would involve making surveys and settling conflicting claims. They also opposed another small-state suggestion that Congress be given sole authority to fix the boundaries in the western lands and create new states from them. The two delegates cast still another negative vote on a provision giving Congress power to regulate commerce and levy taxes. On the matter of apportioning state tax quotas, they supported a proposal that would require the states to feed the common treasury according to "the value of all lands within each State. . . ." They presumed that states like North Carolina with much underdeveloped land would be taxed less than densely populated areas or commercial centers.

When the vitally important question of representation was debated, Harnett and Penn found themselves in different camps. Both voted no on a motion that representation for each state be proportional to the amount of money each contributed to the Confederation. Penn, presumably falling under the influence of the delegates from his native state of Virginia, voted against a resolution giving each state only one vote in Congress and supported two other resolutions calling for representation proportional to population. Harnett, who favored the one-vote arrangement, voted no on the two resolutions in favor of representation on the basis of population. Harnett and the delegates who wanted each state to have one vote won the issue.

Although Harnett and Penn differed on some particular aspects of the Confederation, both were fully committed to the idea of union and were well pleased when they sensed that agreement on the plan would be reached. On November 2 the two delegates from North Carolina excitedly informed Governor Caswell that Congress hoped "to get over the confederation in a fortnight. . . ." While the final vote did not take place until November 15, Harnett was so sure of the outcome that he wrote Thomas Burke on November 13: "The child Congress has been big with these two years past, is at last brought forth." Harnett was afraid that some would think it "deformed," but that Burke would "think it a Monster." After expressing the hope that the state legislatures would act favorably toward the Articles of Confederation, the Wilmington merchant asked that Burke reply with his opinion of the new constitution "freely and dispassionately." Obviously Harnett wanted something from Burke besides the impassioned rhetoric for which he was well known.

More than two weeks after writing Burke, Harnett wrote to William Wilkinson, his friend and business partner in Wilmington, about the recent approval in Congress of the Articles, calling the instrument "the best Confederacy that could be formed, especially when we consider the Number of States, their different Interests, Customs, etc., etc." Harnett expressed satisfaction that state tax quotas for common expenses were to be based on the value of all land under "Patent or Deed" in each state. The "Eastern people," as he called the New Englanders, had wanted a tax quota based on population, which would have included slaves, but this plan, Harnett explained to Wilkinson, "would have ruined poor North Carolina." Besides, a tax quota based on population would not have been equitable, Harnett contended, for North Carolina had almost as many people as Connecticut, but the land of Connecticut, because of its scarcity, was five times as valuable as that of North Carolina.* In short, the richest states, not the most populated ones, should carry the heaviest financial load. At least part of Harnett's gratification over the Confederation seems to have been based on the fact that a union, which to him was in no way detrimental to North Carolina's interests, had won the approval of Congress.

The stand Harnett took in favor of the Confederation was significant for two reasons. First, the struggle to create a union gave Harnett the opportunity to demonstrate that he was more than a provincial leader. He never wavered in his belief in the necessity of forming a union, and he made an intelligent effort to support a plan that would be in the best interest of all the states. While working for the Articles of Confederation in Congress, he skillfully attempted to sell the plan which the Articles embodied to the political leaders back home. Apparently to make North Carolina's influential men feel that they had a part in creating a union, he asked their advice. He wanted to know the sentiment of the members of the General Assembly on the plan

* Population figures for that period are based on contemporary estimates, the accuracy of which is questionable to say the least. Congress's estimates in 1774 for the thirteen colonies as a whole and for most of the individual colonies were highly inflated. The total population of the thirteen colonies was said by Congress to be 3,016,678, but a more realistic figure would be 2,600,000. Congress put North Carolina's total at 300,000, which was probably at least 40,000 too many. Connecticut's population was reckoned to be 192,000 by Congress, and this figure is probably close to being correct. A 1775 estimate, made by someone outside Congress, assigned 200,000 inhabitants to both Connecticut and North Carolina. No one knows what figures Harnett used, but in view of the fact that he believed Connecticut had more people than North Carolina, he could not have used Congress's estimate of 1774.

As far as land area (excluding water-covered areas and western land claims) is concerned, Connecticut had 4,820 square miles, while North Carolina had 48,740 square miles. This means that North Carolina had over ten times as much land as Connecticut. How Harnett decided that Connecticut, with about the same number of people as North Carolina and one-tenth as much land, had land five times more valuable than North Carolina's land is a mystery.

to give each state only one vote. He also asked for some indication of the Assembly's view on the three proposed methods of arriving at tax quotas for each state: (1) by population, (2) by assessing land values, (3) by assessing property in general. Harnett preferred the third method but was willing to compromise and accept the second. Before he voted, however, he invited the opinions of the body which had sent him to Congress. This was good politics and true statesmanship at the same time. Harnett never asked if the North Carolina politicians favored the idea of union, for to that idea he was firmly committed. But he did give the leaders of his state the opportunity to advise him on specific provisions to be included in the constitution. What better way could Harnett have chosen to win for the Confederation the support of men who, he feared, would reject the union as an encroachment on state sovereignty?

The second reason that Harnett's steadfast, forthright stand in favor of the Confederation was important is that he, a tried and true leader for over a decade in the struggle with Great Britain, used his influence to keep John Penn and perhaps the whole General Assembly from concluding with Burke that the Confederation was a "chymerical Project." Harnett, fully aware of Burke's powers of persuasion and certain that political sentiment for state sovereignty abounded in North Carolina, feared that the Articles would meet a hostile reception in his state.

As it turned out, Harnett had good reason to be apprehensive about Burke's opposition, for the fiery Irishman was in North Carolina making plans to prevent, or at least delay, ratification of the Articles by the General Assembly. As a representative of Orange County, Burke attended the meeting of the Assembly in late November, 1777, and there presented his views on state sovereignty and argued for postponing any decision on the Confederation until after the war. Burke's effort to delay adoption of the Articles was partially successful. On December 19 a thirteen-man committee of both houses—a committee on which Burke served—refused to accept the Articles in their existing form, and the Assembly approved the negative report. Thus did Burke carry the day, but his triumph was short-lived.

Harnett, in Pennsylvania, continued to stand firmly for the Articles, letting the leaders of his state know that he disagreed with the recalcitrant Burke. On March 20, 1778, he wrote Governor Caswell and expressed his considered opinion that without the Confederation the door would be "left open for continental Confusion and blood-shed and *that* very soon after we are at peace with Europe." Just over a month later, on April 24, the General Assembly of North Carolina ratified the Articles of Confederation without reservations. After careful consideration the General Assembly, it would seem, decided that the advice of the seasoned revolutionary from Wilmington was to be preferred to that of the brilliant, but young and less experienced Irishman from near Hillsborough.

After the struggle to win North Carolina's acceptance of the Confederation ended in victory, Harnett remained in Congress another year and eight months, continuing to protect the interests of his state and promote the American cause. By the time he left Congress in December, 1779, all the states except Maryland had ratified the Articles of Confederation. In January, 1781, Wilmington was captured by the British, and Harnett fell into Tory hands. He died in April, 1781, while still a captive. By that time Maryland, too, had ratified the nation's new constitution. Harnett must have been pleased to learn, if indeed word ever reached him, that the union he had labored to help create was at last a reality.

4

men,
money,
and materiel
for war

BY THE END of 1777 the vital decisions of the American Revolution had been made. Congress had declared independence and, at least on paper, had formed a union. The deliberations over these two great questions, which were basically philosophical, had given such brilliant and articulate men as William Hooper and Thomas Burke the opportunity to stand out. After 1777 Congress was concerned, not with great philosophical questions, but with practical, day-to-day issues—recruiting soldiers and finding the money to keep them in the field, making alliances with foreign powers, and keeping the channels of trade with Europe open. These matters required less eloquence in debate and more hard work in committee. Consequently, individuals had fewer opportunities to make an impression. This situation, which caused attention to be focused on pressing problems rather than on impressive men, prevailed for the remainder of the war years.

That the Continental Congress—Confederation Congress after March 1, 1781—never completely solved its financial problems is one of the best-known facts of American history. In view of shaky finances the winning of American independence and Congress's success in keeping the young Confederation from collapsing seem almost miraculous. While the financial difficulties that plagued Congress after 1777 are often discussed, they have not been examined in depth through the eyes of the North Carolina delegates or in relationship to North Carolina's simultaneous needs and problems.

When first confronted with a serious need for money, Congress adopted an expedient often used by Americans during colonial days—the liberal issuance of paper money. This money, backed by nothing of substance, was unable to hold its face value for long, and the result was mounting inflation. The North Carolina delegates sympathized with Congress's financial needs but favored taxation rather than emissions of paper money as the best method to raise funds. Perhaps because of the political influence of commercial interests in their home state, the North Carolinians were predisposed to "sound money" or currency that could be redeemed at face value because it was backed by gold or some other commodity of stable value. Thomas Burke had scarcely taken his seat in Congress in 1777 when he called for an end to the emissions of paper money and advocated financial relief through taxation. Almost two years later in December, 1778, he again took a conservative stand on the question of money. A resolution offered in Congress called for the removal from circulation of $41,000,000 in paper currency that had been issued by Congress between May 20, 1777, and April 11, 1778. According to the resolution, these bills had been reproduced by counterfeiters, and the best response Congress could make to that criminal act would be to call the bills in and replace them with loan certificates. Those who stood with Burke against the resolution were in the minority, and the resolution passed.

Joining Burke in opposition to the resolution was Whitmel Hill, a new member of the North Carolina delegation. Hill, one of the most prosperous planters and biggest slaveholders in North Carolina, was from Martin County. He apparently owed his election to Congress to his local prominence derived from his great wealth. His career in Congress would be short and undistinguished.

After he and Burke voted against the loan certificate resolution, they explained their objections in a letter to Governor Caswell. First, the resolution violated North Carolina's rights, since the state had declared the paper money in question to be legal tender, and Congress had no "power to repeal or suspend" state laws. Second, to borrow when money was depreciated would "take ten parts of future Industry to pay for one part of the present, for Loan certificates" would have to "be paid off by appriciated money. . . ." Burke and Hill considered such a method of financing to be unwise and even "Ruinous." Finally, they claimed that the wealthy states would benefit most from the plan.

The negative long-range effects of huge paper-money issues were recognized by Congress by the spring of 1779, and more consideration began to be given to fund-raising methods such as taxing the states and borrowing from foreign countries. Consistently standing by their past position on the question, the North Carolina delegates favored maintaining the public credit through a program of taxation directed by the states. By now this also seemed to be the general mood of Congress. However, Congress refused to close the door on borrowing abroad. Although the North Carolinians did not approve of this method and made that clear to leaders back home, they confessed that they might go along with it if the states did not help Congress raise money. In all probability they feared their state and some others might not be any more generous toward Congress in the future than they had been in the past. Burke was convinced that Congress was struggling to find an acceptable solution to impending financial disaster, but he warned the North Carolina General Assembly that the efforts of Congress would end in failure unless "powerfully aided by Similar Efforts of the

States. . . ." Generally speaking, no such "Similar Efforts" were made in the states, and the financial troubles of Congress steadily increased.

In the months that followed, various Congressmen asserted again and again that America could be saved only by "the exertions of the several States to supply the Continental Treasury." Congress even passed a resolution in October, 1779, asking the states to contribute $15,000,000 monthly and imposing upon them a penalty of six per cent on all deficiencies in payment of their quotas. Cornelius Harnett doubted that the states could contribute $15,000,000 monthly and voted against the resolution. When Congress had previously asked the states for $60,000,000 and, according to Harnett, had received only $3,000,000, he wondered how the states could now be expected to pay $15,000,000 per month. He also objected to North Carolina's quota of $1,000,000 as "out of proportion." The passage of the resolution in addition to talk in Congress about resorting to paper money again greatly disturbed the Wilmington merchant. He was convinced that no more paper money should be issued by Congress or by the states.

In the autumn of 1780 the situation had further deteriorated, at least in the mind of Whitmel Hill. On October 9, concerned about the prospect of a new emission of paper money, he wrote to Burke:

Of these [depreciated bills] the people are quite tired, and when it is to grow better I know not, as I am very apprehensive the new Emission will not have a Circulation when the attempt is made. Are you not exceedingly alarmed at our Situation? Must confess I am exceedingly. Perhaps it may arise from . . . natural Timidity, but the more I reflect on our affairs the more gloomy prospects throw themselves within my view.

A new member of the North Carolina delegation arrived late in December, 1780. Samuel Johnston of Chowan County had

Samuel Johnston

an exalted reputation in North Carolina politics. A man of digni-
fied appearance and olympian attitude, Johnston seemed to in-
spire confidence in his abilities and to attract respect for his
causes. After only a few months in Congress he would be elected
president of that body. Johnston would not accept this honor,
however, because bad health and the need to put his personal
business affairs in order would cause him to resign his seat and
return to North Carolina permanently.

During his six months in Philadelphia Johnston was much
concerned about America's financial plight, which was rapidly
growing more desperate. Johnston did not say much publicly
about the problem during the spring of 1781, but he thought
about it and expressed his ideas to friends. Writing to James
Iredell in April, he likened Congress to a fly entangled in the
"cobweb" of "paper currency"; he said that finances were discussed daily, but all proposals prompted "numberless objections." A month later, on May 8, Johnston reported in another
letter to Iredell that the "great and sudden fall of the old Continental money" had "occasioned very great convulsions and
Dissatisfaction" in Philadelphia and had "reduced all paper
currency to a very doubtful state." He was certain that the
"finances of no country" had ever been "more deranged or more
in want of wisdom and political knowledge to make them effectual." Like other members of Congress, he hoped that Robert
Morris, the new Superintendent of Finance, could find the
remedy.

All the time that Congress struggled with its financial problems, North Carolina, along with some other states, was having
trouble securing needed supplies and materiel of war. The state
had even more difficulty raising troops. The fact is often over-
looked that there were two different American armies during
the Revolutionary War—the Continental Line, which Congress
paid, supplied, and commanded through General George Wash-

ington, and the various state militias, which were responsible
only to their respective states. The Continental Line was composed of a quota of troops from each state. Originally Congress
assigned North Carolina a quota of nine regiments. Each regiment consisted of eight companies of seventy-six men, meaning
that North Carolina was supposed to place a total of 5,472 men
in the Continental Line. Before the end of 1776 another regiment
was added to North Carolina's quota. Enlisting men for the
Continental Line was never easy, mainly because until 1780
North Carolina did not offer a bounty as an inducement to enlist.
Other states recruited vigorously, often crossing state lines to
meet their quotas. When South Carolina had difficulty filling
quotas in 1776, its agents recruited from North Carolina and
Virginia by offering high bounties. By 1779 Virginia offered
four hundred dollars and three hundred acres of land to every
volunteer. North Carolina's bounty law of 1780 provided a payment of five hundred dollars upon enlistment and another five
hundred dollars at the end of each year's service, plus 640 acres
of land. Even after the bounty law was passed, North Carolina's
regiments in the Continental Line *never* had a full complement.

It seems clear that North Carolina's first trouble in enlisting
troops was caused by severely limited funds. Without money,
attractive bounties could not be offered. To solve this problem
the state turned to Congress. Thus when John Penn went to Congress in June, 1777, he went with specific instructions from the
North Carolina legislature to secure funds for the state's use in
recruiting Continental troops. In mid-July, having heard nothing from either Penn or Burke on the matter, Governor Caswell,
in a letter tinged with impatience, wrote to Burke: "I once more
entreat in the most earnest manner that you use your utmost en-
deavors to furnish us with money, without which you know . . .
little can be expected from us." Caswell's letter crossed with a
letter on its way to him containing the good news that Congress
had approved $300,000 for North Carolina.

A Continental infantryman,
First North Carolina Regiment

Even with this rather substantial assistance from Congress, North Carolina could not recruit its share of troops for the Continental Line. About a year after Congress granted the state $300,000, Governor Caswell requested $500,000 more. Little wonder Congress never seemed to have enough money! When Cornelius Harnett and John Penn returned to Congress in September, 1778, after a brief respite, they learned that Congress had approved only one-fifth of the amount that Caswell had requested. They also discovered that Congress had approved only $100,000 because of some members' insistence that North Carolina had already received more than it was due from the Continental treasury. Harnett and Penn were outraged. Penn "loudly complained of it in Congress." Harnett was equally disturbed. Writing to Caswell he said that if he and his associates had been present "the credit of the State . . . would not have been so wantonly sported with." He vowed not to rest until Congress satisfactorily explained its conduct, but at the same time he called upon North Carolina to produce its accounts in order to prove, as he professed to believe, that the Continental treasury was actually indebted to the state. Within a few weeks, because of the efforts of Harnett and Penn, Congress relented and gave North Carolina the remaining $400,000 of the original request. North Carolina, however, made no attempt to produce its accounts.

North Carolina's efforts at military preparedness became more vigorous in 1780, as is evidenced by the passage of the bounty law. This came about because of a dramatic change in British strategy. Until the end of 1778, the British commanders had confined their military activities largely to the middle states, but on December 29 the British captured Savannah, and the main theater of war shifted to the South. Charleston fell in the spring of 1780, and the British general, Lord Cornwallis, then swept across South Carolina. When General Horatio Gates attempted

General Horatio Gates

to stop the British advance, he was routed at Camden on August 16, 1780. Its buffer to the south overrun, North Carolina seemed to lie helpless before a powerful and plundering enemy. In this eleventh hour, North Carolina tried to step up its preparations for war.

The state, at the time of Gates's demoralizing defeat, had four congressional delegates, Thomas Burke, Whitmel Hill, Willie Jones, and William Sharpe. All four—Jones and Hill in Philadelphia and Burke and Sharpe at home for a rest—were horrified at the defeat.

Willie (pronounced Wylie) Jones was a mass of contradictions. Although a tidewater country gentleman, he led the most

Home of Willie Jones in Halifax,
North Carolina

Willie Jones

radical faction in North Carolina politics. Despite his prominence in state politics, he was not outstanding in Congress, and after only six months he would choose to return to the state political environment with which he was more familiar. But in the late summer of 1780, having recently come to Congress, Jones was vocal in his concern over the American disaster at Camden. He wrote to Samuel Johnston lamenting the fact that the North Carolina and Virginia militias had not only refused to fight at Camden, but had abandoned their officers and fled. He considered the defeat, especially in view of the militias' cowardice, "truly alarming." Jones also worried about Whitmel Hill, who might "hang or drown" himself in the event of "another Misfortune to the Southward." Jones's assessment of his colleague's perturbation was accurate, for Hill soon would lead a movement in Congress to investigate General Gates's conduct at Camden.

In October of 1780 Sharpe joined Hill and Jones in Philadelphia. He had previously served in Congress for the last nine months of 1779. Like Burke and Penn, Sharpe was from the so-called "Democratic backcountry." He had been active in Revolutionary politics at both state and local levels and had been an important figure in the Cherokee War of 1776. Having been almost unnoticed in Congress during his first stint, he had despaired of making a contribution and called Congress the "House of Bondage." When at last he began to receive committee assignments, he performed his duties well and became a respected congressman. But immediately following his return to Congress and after Gates's debilitating defeat, he was as discouraged as Jones and Hill and had begun to doubt that America could succeed in its "*great Enterprise.*"

Part of the North Carolina delegates' discouragement in the late summer of 1780 also stemmed from their personal circumstances. Because of spiraling inflation and outrageous prices, the salaries of the delegates had become woefully inadequate, and they often wondered how long they could remain in Philadelphia. Although the North Carolina legislature raised the salaries of the delegates from five hundred pounds "for such portion of their year" as they were "so employed" to eight hundred pounds, then to sixteen hundred pounds by 1778, and ultimately to two thousand pounds before the war ended, the increases never seemed to keep pace with the unrelenting climb in prices. Assuming that the pound was worth approximately five dollars, the delegates during the war years received "$2,500, $4,000, $8,000, and finally $10,000 per year, if they worked a full year. In 1777 expenses for the bare necessities were at least eight dollars a day. But by 1780 the cost of living was out of sight, as can be seen from the records of young James Madison, who arrived in Congress that year. For his first six months in Philadelphia, his board bill was $21,373; laundry, $1,176; the care of his horse, $6,511; liquors, sugar, and fruit, $2,495. If the North Carolina delegates had similar expenses, their salaries did not even cover the cost of food and lodging.

Sharpe urged Burke, who was still in North Carolina, to inform the General Assembly of the delegates' plight. Hill was able to avoid borrowing only by sending home "for a considerable Sum." Jones warned Governor Abner Nash that the three delegates might become "involved in distressing and shameful Circumstances," if the legislature did not hasten to provide adequate financial support. Apparently the financial strain of living in Philadelphia influenced the permanent withdrawal from Congress of both Whitmel Hill and Willie Jones. Both left before the year ended.

Although the North Carolina delegates agonized over Congress's seeming inability to raise money as well as their own personal lack of funds, their primary concern early in 1781 was saving North Carolina from Cornwallis. They worked diligently to acquire arms for the state's militia. On April 26, 1781, Congress ordered "a quantity not exceeding two thousand" muskets to be repaired and sent to North Carolina. The first muskets to be repaired under this order, however, were diverted to Virginia, and then five hundred more of the guns went to Maryland. Finally, on August 30, "one thousand muskets," fifteen hundred "cartouch boxes," and a "quantity of fixed ammunition" were ready for shipment to North Carolina, but Congress's Board of War, upon "the application of Genl. Knox," decided to send these items to the Continental Army in the South. At this point Sharpe, in a letter dated September 1, 1781, appealed to General Washington not to permit arms earmarked for North Carolina to be diverted. If the commander-in-chief allowed this, he would have to take full responsibility for the defense of the state, said Sharpe, for North Carolina was "so destitute of arms" that it could not furnish half its troops and militia with weapons.

Sharpe's letter apparently achieved the desired result, for on December 5, over three months later, another delegate reported to Governor Nash:

> I have obtained from Congress for our State one thousand stand of arms, in addition to the thousand furnished by the Commander in Chief, to be delivered immediately to our [or]der at Richmond with Cartridge boxes, Flints, Cartridges, powder and Musket Ball, in proportion to the muskets, tho I hope by this time you do not need them. . . .

By then North Carolina did not need them. Cornwallis, after threatening the state through much of 1781, had surrendered at Yorktown, Virginia, in October. On the other hand, it was too soon to take final victory for granted. The British still held Wilmington and Charleston.

As a result of Congress's cutting back on ordering supplies and of the negotiation of foreign loans by Robert Morris, the American financial picture brightened, at least temporarily, late

Hugh Williamson

in 1781. For nearly a year optimism ran high. Then, beginning in October, 1782, and continuing until peace was formally achieved, money troubles again plagued Congress. In these closing months of the war, three new North Carolina delegates, Hugh Williamson, Benjamin Hawkins, and William Blount, were to endure the same frustrations that the delegates of 1780 had known.

Williamson was easily the most outstanding of the three men. He was a true eighteenth-century man, more learned than Hooper, more versatile than Burke. Jefferson remembered Williamson for his diligence, his "acute mind," and his "erudition." As a young man he had spent a short time in the ministry, then had taught mathematics at the College of Philadelphia while he studied medicine. Eventually he had gone to Europe and earned his medical degree at the University of Utrecht. Not long after returning to America to practice medicine, he found that his delicate health caused him to contract the diseases of the patients he treated. Consequently, he gave up his practice except as a sideline.

Deciding to become a merchant, he moved to Charleston and finally to Edenton, North Carolina, where he built up a lucrative trade with the French West Indies. His occasional practice of medicine led to his becoming surgeon-general of all North Carolina's troops in the state. In 1782 Edenton elected Williamson to the North Carolina General Assembly, which chose him as a delegate to the Confederation Congress. As a member of Congress he lacked Burke's intensity, but not his indefatigability. By the time the doctor-merchant arrived, standing boards had been abandoned, but committees were still being appointed to handle every conceivable kind of business. Williamson set a scorching pace, serving on eighty-five committees in one year. Grinding as the daily routine must have been, Williamson almost never missed a day at his post, and he never complained.

Not since Burke and Hooper had North Carolina been so ably represented.

Williamson's two colleagues were another matter. Hawkins had some ability. He seldom entered into the debates, but he certainly did his share of committee work and in this way earned the respect of his fellow congressmen. His major contributions to the nation as an Indian agent, however, would come after the war, not during it. William Blount was among the weakest men North Carolina sent to Congress during the war years. He had nothing to say in the debates and served on few committees. Like Hawkins, he would occupy important elective and appointive offices after the war. He would also be expelled from the United States Senate and end his political career under a dark cloud.

When these new delegates arrived in Philadelphia at the end of 1782, they found Congress's financial situation to be critical. In October Blount and Williamson reported to Governor Alexander Martin that Congress had to find ways to support the public credit, raise money for the next year, and find money to meet the expenses of the current year. Congress, they said, planned to borrow, if possible, $5,000,000 from France or Holland. Some in Congress advocated substantial taxes to avoid borrowing money at high rates of interest, but Williamson and Blount—of all things for North Carolina delegates to do—favored borrowing on the ground that North Carolina was not able, under existing circumstances, to pay taxes. North Carolina's staples were too bulky for shipping in time of war; thus the state's way to make money with which to pay taxes was temporarily restricted.

By March, 1783, Congress was confronted with another money crisis. The army was demanding its pay, as were "all other public Creditors." Williamson and Blount informed Governor Martin that Congress had pledged the army a month's pay and had promised to find some way to fund the public debt. However, both the army and the creditors, they assured Martin, were becoming anxious for "something more substantial" than promises. So bad was the financial state that Robert Morris, a few weeks earlier, had informed Congress that he would resign as treasurer at the end of May unless adequate steps were taken to bring in necessary revenue. Expecting momentarily "to adopt a system of Finance which might revive the public credit," Congress ignored Morris's threat to resign. Apparently irked at Congress's failure to respond to his tentative resignation, Morris wrote and released to the newspapers a letter in which he bluntly accused the states of showing no "disposition" to "provide funds." The North Carolina delegates thought the letter "incautiously worded," and stated that it might have been damaging "if the public credit had been alive." But, they lamented, "there are times when nothing can hurt."

Hopeless as the situation looked, Congress continued its struggle to find an acceptable way to raise money. On April 18, 1783, a decision was reached to revive the proposal for an impost—a proposal similar to one that the Rhode Island delegates had almost singlehandedly blocked in 1781. This time Congress, in effect, asked for an amendment to the Articles of Confederation. Ratification of this amendment would have given Congress authority to levy specific duties on a variety of designated imported articles and a duty of five per cent ad valorem on all other imports. The states were to choose the collectors of the duties, but, once named by the states, the collectors were to answer to Congress. In addition to the impost, Congress asked the states to contribute $1,500,000 a year, with each state paying a prescribed quota, until a tax structure in accordance with Article VIII of the Articles of Confederation could be devised. Furthermore, Congress asked that steps be taken to amend Article VIII so that state contributions would be proportional to population rather than based on land value. Rhode Island, once more the spoiler, immediately attacked the proposed amendment, and several

LIBRARY
WAYNE STATE COLLEGE
WAYNE, NEBRASKA

other states were willing to accept the plan only with certain restrictions.

During the time when Congress was devising a method to fill its empty treasury, the army, having heard that a peace agreement was all but made, grew restless to be discharged. But the soldiers did not intend to go home without money in their pockets, and Washington warned Congress that less than three months' pay per man might provoke serious trouble. Congress, working with Morris, who had agreed to stay at his post a while longer, passed stopgap measures in April and May, 1783. The soldiers would be paid in notes issued in anticipation of revenue from the states. According to the plan, the men would receive three months' pay and be furloughed until the definitive peace treaty arrived. Then they would be discharged. Unfortunately, at the time designated for the furloughs to begin, the notes were not available for distribution. Most of the soldiers, though probably disgusted and disappointed, simply trudged off home without creating a disturbance. Some, however, notably several hundred troops from the Pennsylvania and Maryland lines, threatened mutiny at Lancaster and Philadelphia. Two incidents, occurring on June 13 and June 21, resulted in Congress's removal to Princeton, New Jersey. From that place on August 1, 1783, Williamson and Hawkins wrote Governor Martin a full report of what had happened. Their comments on the reasons for the disturbances are most interesting:

We had nothing to fear from the disposition of our Army, provided they could have been paid; but we believe there never was an instance of an army being kept together who were so ill paid as ours, much less of their being disbanded without pay. Congress have long viewed the present as a dreadful crisis which must prove truly alarming to the peace and liberty of our Country, unless effectual payment could be made to the troops. The conduct of some of the States put it out of our power to borrow money and we need not add, that the States have not enabled us by their own exertions to pay the army or any other creditors.

Remarkably enough, the spirit of mutiny soon subsided, and on October 19 Williamson and Hawkins wrote Martin that the army was no more. All "officers and Soldiers" had been furloughed.

The fact that Williamson's and Hawkins's sympathies were with the unpaid troops is better understood when it is noted that they themselves were not being paid. The North Carolina delegates of 1780 and 1781 had complained because their salaries did not keep pace with inflation. By the fall of 1783 the North Carolina delegates were not even receiving their salaries. In a letter of September 27, 1783, Hawkins expressed his dissatisfaction with having to remain so long at his post without relief and "without support from the State." He wrote:

I have for some time been absolutely without as much money as will support me one day except what I borrow and perhaps may not be able to repay. Surely it can never comport with the dignity of a Sovereign State, to let their Delegates depend on such humiliating and precarious means of support.

Less than a month later, on October 19, Hawkins, joined by Williamson, wrote Martin again. If their situation had changed at all, it had been for the worse. They were without "one shilling of money." None of their colleagues had arrived to give them respite, and no word of when to expect financial relief had reached them. Trying to shame the governor, they asserted that all state treasurers paid their delegates regularly by the month except North Carolina's. Consequently, said Williamson and Hawkins, the North Carolina delegates had to "depend on borrowing" for their "decent support." Apprehensive that their credit would soon "be like the remittances" of their state, the

two delegates asked the governor to determine how such han-
dling of affairs could "comport with the dignity of a Sovereign
State."

Thus did the war end as it had begun—with Congress and
North Carolina virtually insolvent. Congress had the money, or
more accurately the credit, to pay its soldiers only a fraction of
what was due, and North Carolina was not even paying its delegates in Congress. The financial situation was indeed bleak, but
it had not been much better during the eight long years of war.
And yet, somehow, Congress, the nation it represented, and the
individual states had endured.

5

trying
to turn land
into money

DURING THE MONTHS following the great American victory at Yorktown, expenses continued to mount, and Congress, despite its long and desperate search for money, seemed no closer to a solution of its financial problems than it had been in 1777 or 1778. Aside from unpopular taxes, there appeared to be only one untapped source of revenue left—the western lands claimed by some of the states. If the states having claims on lands beyond the Appalachian Mountains would cede their holdings to Congress, then, reasoned some, Congress could survey and sell the land and thereby create a major source of revenue for the Confederation. As more and more members of Congress were attracted to this point of view, the pressure upon the landed states to cede their western land became increasingly intense.

The question of what to do about western land was by no means new, but the idea of using it to produce revenue for Congress certainly was a new emphasis. When the question had first come up in 1777, it had been more a political issue than anything else. States having no claims to western land, led by Maryland, had not wanted the states which did have such claims to augment their political power by promoting settlement and extending their jurisdiction over the western lands. The states without land claims wanted the landed states to cede control of their unsettled territories to Congress. States that claimed trans-

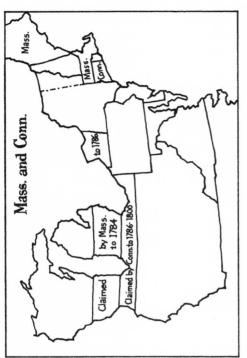

Mass. and Conn.

Mass.

Mass.
Conn.

to 1786

Claimed
by Mass.
to 1784

Claimed by Conn. to 1786-1800

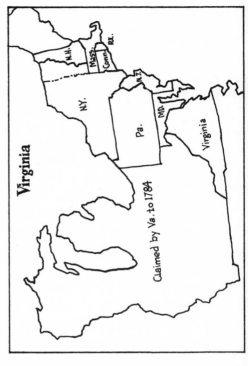

Virginia

N.H.
Mass.
Conn.
R.I.

N.Y.

Pa.

N.J.
MD.

Virginia

Claimed by Va. to 1784

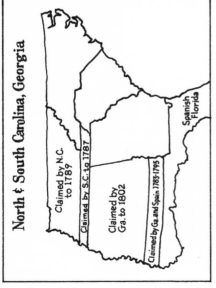

North & South Carolina, Georgia

Claimed by N.C.
to 1789

Claimed by S.C. to 1787

Claimed by
Ga. to 1802

Claimed by Ga. and Spain 1783-1795

Spanish
Florida

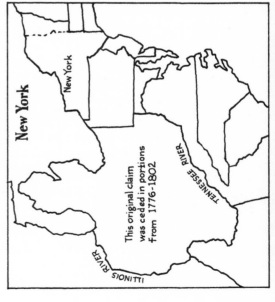

New York

New York

This original claim
was ceded in portions
from 1776-1802

ILLINOIS RIVER

TENNESSEE RIVER

montane land on the basis of their old colonial charters were Massachusetts, Connecticut, Virginia, North Carolina, South Carolina, and Georgia. New York asserted its right of ownership in the Great Lakes region on the ground that the Iroquois Indians, who lived in the area, had long been under New York's jurisdiction. Massachusetts and Connecticut had sea-to-sea grants and consequently claimed strips as wide as their respective states from the western boundary of New York to the Pacific Ocean; but Massachusetts's claim conflicted with those of New York and Virginia; and Connecticut's claim conflicted with those of Pennsylvania and Virginia. Virginia had by far the largest claim, for it included present-day West Virginia (which at that time was a part of the state of Virginia), Kentucky, Ohio, Indiana, Illinois, Michigan, and Wisconsin, plus land west of the Mississippi River stretching to the Pacific. However, Massachusetts, Connecticut, and Virginia showed no inclination to press their claims to lands west of the Mississippi. North Carolina claimed the area which is now Tennessee, and Georgia claimed most of what today are the states of Alabama and Mississippi. South Carolina claimed a narrow strip of land about fourteen miles wide extending from its present western tip to the Mississippi River.

Having no claims at all to western lands were New Hampshire, Rhode Island, Pennsylvania, New Jersey, Delaware, and Maryland. The demand by Maryland that all western lands be ceded to Congress before that state would approve the Articles of Confederation had blocked ratification of the Articles for at least two years, but Maryland had not succeeded in forcing the cession of *all* western lands. When Maryland had finally ratified the Articles in 1781, only New York had given up all the western land it had once claimed, while Connecticut and Virginia had made partial cessions to Congress.

Between 1777 and 1782 the North Carolina delegates generally opposed any sort of cession, full or partial, by the state. Late in October, 1779, a majority of Congress had proposed that Virginia "put a stop to the further granting of Vacant Lands until the Conclusion of the War." This action had been designed to lure Maryland into ratifying the Articles of Confederation, but Cornelius Harnett and William Sharpe had joined Virginia in voting against the proposal. Harnett understood the unlanded states' fear that western settlement could be used to increase the political leverage of the landed states, but he was beginning to see more at stake than political power in the land controversy. Although the supporters of the resolution had claimed that they only wanted to prevent settlers from occupying the land during turbulent times, Harnett suspected that they really wanted to prepare the way for Congress to appropriate all western lands and sell them to pay off the public debt after the war. If this was the objective of the supporters of the resolution, they concealed it, but both Harnett and Sharpe remained convinced that their state's own land claims were somehow in jeopardy. Some members of Congress were already contending that the western lands of the various states had passed from state jurisdiction to congressional control. The two North Carolina delegates rejected that position and announced in a letter to Governor Richard Caswell that they were determined to oppose any congressional measures taking North Carolina lands, unless the General Assembly instructed them otherwise. In their minds, the states that had no claims to western land were jealous of Virginia and North Carolina.

Joining Harnett and Sharpe in the fight to protect North Carolina's western land were Thomas Burke and Willie Jones. In March, 1780, Burke was assigned to a committee to consider an act of the New York legislature which had turned over to Congress *a portion* of western land claimed by that state. The committee, unable to agree on a course of action, was soon dissolved.

While the evidence is not conclusive, it suggests that Burke opposed New York's action. In all probability he thought that such a step would set a precedent potentially dangerous to the interests of North Carolina. Willie Jones could also see good reasons for North Carolina's holding on to its western land, at least for the time being. When the issue was hotly debated in Congress during the summer of 1780, Jones served on a committee which, on September 6, recommended a liberal surrender of western lands claimed by the landed states. Obviously Jones did not support the recommendation, for on October 1, he wrote to Governor Abner Nash as follows: "I think it will be time enough for No. Carolina to deliberate on the surrender of Western Territory, when the states have vigorously supported and finally secured her [i.e., defended her against Cornwallis's advancing army] in her Eastern Territory. . . ." Jones, then, favored no cession of western land by North Carolina until the British were no longer a threat to the state.

The strange thing about Burke's opposition to cession was that, by this time, he was showing a real concern for national problems and privately might have favored his state's ceding its western land. Publicly he consistently stood against cession because he knew that the North Carolina General Assembly meant to keep its "Tennessee Country." He knew why the legislators viewed the matter as they did, and he respected their position. He explained the attitude of the North Carolina lawmakers in a letter written late in 1780 to the South Carolinian John Laurens, soldier, diplomat, and son of the famous Henry Laurens. North Carolina, Burke pointed out to Laurens, could hardly be expected to give its western land to Congress while other states, which were wealthier than North Carolina, retained "all their more Valuable property entire and unaffected by such a Constitution [Articles of Confederation]." In other words, if the Articles were never ratified and no machinery was ever set up to collect taxes

A frontiersman and a plowman

from all the states under the tax formula spelled out in Article VIII, then the landed states would end up giving a great deal in the general interest, while the states without western land would conceivably give nothing. Burke wanted safeguards against this potential inequity.

The first signs that North Carolina's congressional representatives were softening on the issue of land cession appeared in October, 1782, when Hugh Williamson and William Blount warned Governor Alexander Martin that pressure in favor of cession was steadily building up in Congress. Since the Articles of Confederation had been ratified for a year and a half, the advocates of cession, who were from the "smaller States and some of the larger ones," could no longer base their position on the need to secure ratification. Now they openly admitted that they were interested in the western lands as a source of revenue. Rhode Island, a state which had refused to approve the five per cent impost on trade as a means of raising revenue, was eager for the landed states to turn their western lands over to Congress for that purpose. Williamson and Blount were convinced that Rhode Island's position was "contrary to the express terms of Confederation." They believed that North Carolina should use revenues from its western land to pay off *state* debts. Although the most recent resolution in Congress to force the states to cede their western lands had been defeated, the delegates predicted that the question would recur and again be "the subject of warm and obstinate contention" when the "Northern and Minor States" were "better represented." They suggested that North Carolina might be able to work out an acceptable compromise that would protect its interests on the one hand and demonstrate its spirit of cooperation on the other. This did not mean that the two delegates liked the idea of cession. They still favored raising revenues through taxes and were determined to work for a tax program based on Article VIII. Up to this time no steps had been taken to establish a tax system based on the eighth article because the British had controlled large areas of the country. Now that the British threat was rapidly vanishing, the two North Carolina delegates suspected that some of the states, particularly those in New England, were craftily trying to avoid a "Federal Quota" by selling somebody else's land to raise the needed revenues.

Williamson and Blount realized that their plan to work out a tax system would probably not be accepted and that the cession of western lands would be insisted upon as an alternative means of raising money. Therefore, they offered a plan for giving up the "Tennessee Country" under conditions that would make the cession advantageous to North Carolina. They set forth five conditions that the state might insist upon: (1) that in determining any tax quota for North Carolina, Congress should give credit for the campaign against the Cherokee Indians the state had undertaken in 1776; (2) that an "actual valuation" should be made by Congress "of all lands and their improvements claimed by any State" before the cession could be confirmed; (3) that there should be a clarification of all state accounts in order to separate the Confederation debt from state debts; (4) that lands ceded should be disposed of in a way that would best pay off the public debt and that this course be determined by agreement of nine or more states; and (5) that in the event a new state was formed from any ceded lands, "part of the public debt" should be "transferred to such State according to land values." These five conditions represented a shrewd scheme. If the North Carolina delegates could not obtain a favorable vote in Congress for a tax program based on Article VIII, they would attempt to force Congress to accept elements of such a program by incorporating them into the set of conditions upon which North Carolina would cede its western land!

The following month Williamson wrote Martin again, urging him to ask the General Assembly to turn its attention to the

"Western Country" because the "Spirit of Migration" and "making new States" had reached "epidemic" proportions. The small states, argued the Congressman, envied the landed states and were determined "to make us all of the Pigmy breed." He had heard that troublemakers were encouraging the transmontane settlers to revolt against the states which claimed jurisdiction over them and to establish their own independent states. Williamson knew already of a movement to erect a state in the "back of Virginia." Convinced that the source of the turmoil was land speculators and not the settlers themselves, the doctor-merchant urged North Carolina officials to head off any such movement in the "Tennessee Country" so that North Carolina's western "Subjects" would be "among the last to run riot." Unless the North Carolina legislature acted to enforce its jurisdiction, the state's western land might be lost, Williamson warned.

For the next year the pressures for cession continued to build. The western settlers who were supposedly under the jurisdiction of North Carolina and Virginia grew increasingly restless, pushing for independence and statehood. Apparently the North Carolina legislature did nothing about Williamson's warning. Although the settlers in the "Tennessee Country" did not yet go so far as did some settlers west of Pennsylvania and actually declare themselves a state, they were beginning to think along those lines, and that continued to trouble Williamson. In addition, Virginia had already offered its western lands to Congress, on certain conditions, and gradually during 1783 an acceptable compromise was worked out between Congress and Virginia. North Carolina, often attacked as a state doing less than its share, was beginning to appear as a stubborn holdout (one of the last) on the cession issue.

Under these circumstances the North Carolina delegates began to see cession differently. In September, 1783, Williamson and Benjamin Hawkins pointed out to Governor Martin that all

lands ceded by the state would be sold to raise the funds needed
to pay off the army and the other Confederation debts and that
North Carolina would, therefore, benefit indirectly from the
lands already ceded by Virginia and New York. They recommended that North Carolina go ahead and cede part of its western land to the United States on the conditions suggested earlier.
Arguing that the state might "save more by the conditions" than
it would ever realize in revenue from selling land, they claimed
to be "not a little embarrassed" by their state's refusal to make
even a partial cession.

Governor Martin replied to them on December 8, 1783, and
what he had to say must have caused them further embarrass-

ment. He reported that North Carolina had rejected the idea of cession and planned to sell its western land to raise money for the state. The General Assembly had created the new county of Davidson on the Cumberland River, and the lands within its boundaries had been set aside for the soldiers of North Carolina's Continental Line. The rest of the "Tennessee Country" was available to any North Carolinian or American who would pay the state land agent £10 (about fifty dollars) in gold or silver per hundred acres. North Carolina currency, which was called specie certificates and was backed by gold or silver, could also be used to pay for the land, as could Continental money, but it took eight hundred dollars in Continental currency to equal one dol-

A frontier wedding

lar in gold or silver. To discourage rampant speculation, the amount of land one purchaser could buy was restricted to 5,000 acres. The governor defended the legislature's new policy with respect to the state's western land, for he believed that North Carolina needed to hold on to its land until its "own internal debt was paid." In his mind, the sale of that land was the only way the state could discharge its large debt (of perhaps several million dollars). He conjectured that the good land would probably sell quickly and that there would be no acceptable land left to cede to the Confederation.

Thus the year 1783 ended without North Carolina's making any kind of cession to Congress, but that body would not give up and kept applying pressure until the state at last yielded. In April, 1784, the North Carolina General Assembly passed the Cession Act. The western land, by the terms of this law, was to be turned over to Congress subject to some conditions, but the conditions did not include a demand, as Williamson had urged, that Congress implement a tax system based on Article VIII. Consequently, Hugh Williamson opposed the act, arguing that it did not give "adequate protection to North Carolina." He, with the help of William R. Davie and other influential state leaders, was able to secure the repeal of the Cession Act in October, 1784. Governor Martin, in a letter dated December 4, 1784, notified the president of Congress that the North Carolina General Assembly had taken back the state's western land. This did not mean, the governor explained, that the state objected to contributing its share to the public debt, for at the same time the Assembly had repealed the Cession Act it had levied a tax to help Congress pay the interest on the Confederation's foreign debt. That tax, Martin assured Congress, would be "collected with the State Taxes and remitted to Congress." Another letter by the governor, dated the same day, made a similar report to the North Carolina delegation in Congress.

Although the position on western land taken by North Carolina and its congressional delegates can be understood, it is unfortunate that the state's provincial outlook prevented its following the example of Virginia and the northern states in giving up some land for the common cause. The intransigence of North Carolina on the land issue added weight to charges of selfishness already directed against the state and, in the long run, may have been more damaging than the loss of western land. Not until 1789 would North Carolina finally cede its western land to the United States, and by that time a government formed under the new Constitution of 1787 would have taken the place of the Confederation. The way would be prepared at last for a happy ending to the issue of the lands which had been a source of controversy for so long. In 1796 North Carolina's western land would become the state of Tennessee.

6

the
long search
for peace

DURING THOSE LAST YEARS of the war, at the same time
Congress was wrestling with the troublesome questions of money
and western land, there was strong sentiment in the Congress
for negotiating a peace agreement in order to end the fighting
with Great Britain as quickly as possible. Although serious negotiations did not begin until after the surrender of Lord Cornwallis to General Washington at Yorktown on October 19,
1781, the idea of settling the war at the peace table had been
discussed much earlier and had provoked controversy in Congress during 1779. As might be expected, Thomas Burke could
be found in the thick of the dispute about what acceptable terms
of peace would be.

By early 1779 Burke had earned the respect, if not the love,
of his congressional colleagues, and he was appointed to the
highly important committee to recommend preliminary peace
objectives. On February 23, in its report to Congress, the committee urged that the United States insist upon the right to
navigate the Mississippi River freely and that it demand rein-
statement of a right that Americans had formerly enjoyed—
the right to fish off Canadian shores. Burke undoubtedly had opposed part of the report in committee, for on the floor of Congress
he spoke against the insistence upon fishing rights. He argued

that it was not worthwhile to prolong the war for "that object." Burke's objection was brushed aside in the final vote, which included the provision for fishing rights. The vote, taken on July 29, was strictly sectional. Maryland and the states to the south of it voted no, while the states from Delaware to New Hampshire, led by the New Englanders, voted yes. Agreement over the navigation of the Mississippi River was reached by a majority of Congress on September 17, 1779. Ten days later Congress chose John Adams of Massachusetts and John Jay of New York to serve as peace commissioners. They would, when the opportunity arose, enter into negotiations with England.

America's search for peace, thus begun, continued with little progress for three years. Samuel Johnston wrote from Philadelphia on June 23, 1781, to Thomas Burke: "You will before this reaches you have heard that a Negociation for peace is on foot in Europe under the Mediation of the Emperor and Empress Queen of Russia. . . ." If Johnston was optimistic, he should not have been, for more than another year would pass without anything happening except the spread of more rumors.

By August, 1782, Philadelphia buzzed with talk of impending peace negotiations. The North Carolina delegates then in Congress, Hugh Williamson and William Blount, did not have very high hopes. In their minds the British were playing tricks, and they made this point clear in a letter to Governor Alexander Martin:

It is our duty to inform your Excellency that the sending [of] our prisoners to America [by the British] at this Juncture is not by any means a clear proof of benevolence, it may with equal probability be passed to the Acct. of cunning: for the enemy wish and expect regular Soldiers in exchange for those people, many of whom are neither Soldiers nor sailors. There is certainly a disposition in the present English Ministry to excite among the people of America some desire of a Separate peace.

The British, in other words, were trying to exchange American civilians for British soldiers and were also working to cause a rift in the Franco-American Alliance. Williamson and Blount advocated a firm stand until the enemy was prepared to accept reasonable terms.

Two months later, on October 22, the two North Carolina delegates were still suspicious of the British. Convinced that, as in the past, Britain would never give Americans "anything but hard measures," the two North Carolinians contended that Britain should be watched closely. They were certain that the British ministry had such "a vindictive hostile disposition towards America" that it "would gladly embrace any encouragement to repeat their attempts at Conquest."

At the same time the delegates made known their suspicions about the British, they confidently maintained that America's ally, France, would protect American interests. Arthur Lee of Virginia, the leader of an anti-Gallican group in Congress, objected to the instructions Congress gave to the American peace commissioners because those instructions compelled the commissioners to work too closely with the French in the negotiations. When Lee rose in Congress on August 8, 1782, and moved that "the instructions given on the 15 June 1781 to the ministers plenipotentiary for negotiating the peace be reconsidered," Hugh Williamson opposed the motion. According to Lee, the instructions were a source of potential danger to the United States, but the North Carolina delegate said that he could not see anything dangerous about the instructions. He argued that the American envoys were authorized to confer with France only on such lesser matters as boundaries and fishing rights, not on the vital issue of the "independence of the States." A vigorous debate ensued, and in the end Lee's efforts to change the instructions failed.

Throughout the war years the North Carolina delegation remained determined to stand by America's alliance with France. In 1778 France had formally agreed to allow Americans to send raw materials to the French West Indies. Wartime conditions had inhibited trade, but on September 26, 1783, Williamson and Hawkins wrote Governor Martin that they believed France would help develop American commerce by opening the French West Indies to America. In 1784 France reconfirmed its earlier agreement to allow trading privileges, and Americans began a lively trade with the French West Indies. Unfortunately for France, American merchants would use the profits from this trade to purchase English, instead of French, manufactured goods.

By the end of 1782, some members of Congress began to feel that the prospects for beginning serious peace negotiations were good. John Taylor Gilman, a New Hampshire delegate, said in a letter dated December 17 that the "latest accounts from Eu-

View of a West Indies Harbor, published in 1782

rope" indicated that "Negociations for Peace" would be seriously entered upon soon. And on January 7, 1783, William Blount wrote his brother, John Gray Blount, that Richard Oswald had been empowered by the British government on September 21, 1782, "to treat for and conclude with the Commissioners of the Thirteen United States of North America . . . a Truce or Peace." Blount said that he expected the negotiations to take time, but that he believed they would result in peace, which he, for one, "fervently" desired. Thomas Blount, William's brother who lived in Tarborough, was not quite so optimistic. On March 2, 1783, writing to John Gray Blount, he remarked: "Billy [i.e., William] Blount went from here this morning homewards, has been 37 days from Phil[a] & knows no more of peace or War than you, I, & everybody else do, but thinks probability in favor of peace."

William Blount

On March 24, 1783, Williamson and Hawkins joyfully sent word to Governor Martin that on January 20 past "the preliminaries for a general Peace were signed by all the belligerent Powers." They were ecstatic, and they, along with Governor Martin, began an anxious vigil for news of the "definitive Treaty." Their vigil lasted much longer than they expected. On August 4, Williamson wrote the governor that the treaty had been "strangely delayed." However, he said there was reason to believe that the treaty had been signed in Paris on May 27 and that a copy of it would arrive any day.

By August 23 Williamson's optimism had turned to gloom and uncertainty. He and Hawkins wrote Martin that, after Congress had accepted the "provisional Treaty," some difficulties had arisen over certain conditions. British troops had orders to evacuate their posts in America, but only after Congress gave assurance that there would be no reprisals against Loyalists once the troops were gone. Even if Congress did ask the states to give such assurances, it would take time to receive their responses, and further time would be needed for the British to complete their preparations for evacuation, the delegates explained. Consequently, Congress had resolved not to "forward the Treaty to the several States" until further word about acceptance of the definitive treaty was heard from Paris. Williamson and Hawkins also worried about a rumor that Lord North would return to power and try to "embarrass the proceedings." Moreover, reports had arrived from England which indicated that the British had changed their minds about their earlier offer of "perfect reciprocity" in Anglo-American commercial relations. Unless Congress could "interpose" in such a way as to undo this damage, no treaty satisfactory to and binding upon all the states would be worked out, Williamson and Hawkins warned.

By late September the two delegates had gained a clearer picture of what had happened, and they explained everything in a long report to Governor Martin. No progress had been made since hostilities had ended and the preliminary treaty had been signed, and American citizens were the cause of it. Hoping to monopolize American trade and close out the French and Dutch, the British had "courted" American "affections" by offering "terms of perfect reciprocity." Then the British ministry had fallen and two months had passed before another one had been formed. During this period peace negotiations had come to a standstill, but trade had not. American ports had been thrown open "to everything that was called British," and American vessels, especially, had "crowded into British ports in a manner astonishing to all Europe." As a result, Britain had changed the "terms first offered" so that Americans would "have no trade with the West Indies, & very little with Great Britain itself [other] than to import their goods." For this unhappy turn of events Williamson and Hawkins blamed greedy northern merchants, especially those of Philadelphia. Pennsylvania's delegates in Congress had urged "with indecent importunity" some congressional measure approving British trade in American ports. The southern members in Congress had blocked the attempt to pass such a measure, but some states had opened their ports anyway, and the "disease soon became general." Exceedingly irked at the northern states, the two North Carolina delegates lamented the "palpable defect in the Federal Government" which made it possible for Congress to make treaties but not to restrain commerce "so as to cause those Treaties to be observed."

Another report went out from Williamson and Hawkins to Governor Martin on October 19, 1783. Their worst fears had been confirmed. Lord North now headed the British government and would agree to give the United States nothing more than "virtual and substantial reciprocity" rather than "literal reciprocity." The North Carolina delegates considered this latest offer to be "shadow" and not "substance." A "confidential person to

Lord North

the President of Congress," according to the delegates, had discussed the matter with Lord North, who had assumed an unyielding stance on the question of American commerce. The Prime Minister had claimed that Britain could not open the British West Indies to American ships without violating Britain's Navigation Acts, which stated that goods entering or leaving American colonies must be carried on British ships. When threatened that Americans would retaliate by not allowing their goods to go to those islands in British ships, North had admitted that the United States had every right to adopt such a policy. He had been quick to point out, however, that to do so would hurt American trade much more than it would "injure Great Britain." Lord North had ended the discussion by saying that he saw no chance of a commercial treaty between Great Britain and the United States for a long time because Congress could not enforce a trade agreement and the "several States probably would not ratify or observe it." In view of this reported conversation, Williamson and Hawkins dejectedly concluded that the "definitive Treaty" would probably be "a *Verbatim Transcript* of the provisional articles with the necessary alterations of preamble, &c." but without the inclusion of specific trading policies. They promised to send the governor more information when it became available.

Gnawing doubts plagued the North Carolina delegates as they waited anxiously in late October for further word on the treaty. Finally, on November 1, Williamson wrote John Gray Blount that the "definitive Treaty" had been signed on September 3— "on which I give you Joy." John Adams's secretary, Williamson informed Blount, had left France on September 20 to bring the treaty to Congress for ratification. Under the Articles of Confederation, the concurrence of nine states, a two-thirds majority of the thirteen states, was required to pass any important measure, such as the peace treaty. The treaty agreement also specified that ratification had to occur in Congress and the document be returned to England within six months. If this deadline could not be met, all the treaty agreements would have to be negotiated again. On December 5 Williamson wrote William Blount that the North Carolina delegates expected Congress to ratify the treaty "in a fortnight."

More than a fortnight passed, but the ratification did not take place. There was not a sufficient number of state delegations assembled in Congress to call a vote and obtain the necessary two-thirds majority. Richard Dobbs Spaight, appointed to Congress by Governor Martin to fill the unexpired term of William Blount, who had resigned, assumed his new post on December 17. A native of New Bern, Spaight had served many terms in the General Assembly. Affable and highly regarded by his contemporaries, he would, the next year, be duly elected to Congress and serve two terms as a valuable representative, occasionally entering the debates and doing his share of committee work. Spaight was pessimistic about ratification as he wrote to Blount soon after his arrival:

The definitive treaty is to be ratified & exchanged in six Months, four of which are nearly elapsed; the prospect of having Nine States in Congress in a short period is not verry great—I am afraid the British will have it in their power either to Accept, or refuse the Treaty as they may think fit, for it don't appear to me probable that it will be ratified and exchanged in the limitted time.

Among those who might have been just as glad if the treaty had not been ratified was North Carolina's governor. Martin was upset that the treaty did not mention American trade in the British West Indies. Although Anglo-American commerce had been discussed time and time again during the negotiations, the definitive treaty ignored the subject—mainly because the British ministries that rose and fell during those months of negotiation were badly divided on the issue. Martin feared—correctly—that the treaty's silence on the question of trade with the British West Indies meant that the islands had been closed to America. He expressed to the delegates the view that the states should act in concert and speedily retaliate against British trade with America, the volume of which, he observed, was growing daily.

Since Martin's letter expressing his opinions was dated January 21, 1784, he probably did not know when he wrote that Congress had finally ratified the treaty on January 14. Until that time there had not been enough states with representatives in Congress to take a vote.

Not until March 19 did Hugh Williamson write the governor to explain all the circumstances that had surrounded ratification. He admitted that near the end of December he had become extremely apprehensive lest Britain offer "less palatable" terms in the event a new treaty had to be negotiated. Therefore, he had been "one of those who would have submitted to the risque of ratifying by seven States rather than lose the Treaty." Convinced that the treaty was needed to "preserve the peace and happiness of his country," he had stood ready, if nine state delegations had not soon gathered, to risk "his political existence or even his temporal existence."

At this time Williamson, along with James Madison of Virginia and Elbridge Gerry of Massachusetts, served on a very important committee which was responsible for advising Congress about instructions to American diplomatic agents in foreign countries. If ratification had not been accomplished, it would have become the duty of this committee to suggest to Congress new negotiating terms and instructions for their diplomatic agents. Through Williamson's membership on this committee, it may be inferred that he was greatly concerned with the issue of peace and as well informed on the subject as was possible under existing circumstances.

Williamson also reported to Governor Martin that the "officers" that Congress had dispatched to Paris with the completed ratification were delayed by "ice and bad weather" and expressed the concern of Congress that the men might not reach Paris on time, for "the 3d of March was the last day allowed for the exchange of ratification." Although Williamson probably did not know it at the time he wrote this letter, the officers had still not reached the French capital. In fact, they would not arrive until the end of March—too late to fall within the previously agreed-upon deadline of six months. The British ministry, however, showed no inclination to make an issue of their late arrival and accepted the ratification.

And so the long struggle with Great Britain ended. Independence, the American objective since July 2, 1776, had been won. Congress had done an admirable job in uniting and leading the American people to a successful conclusion of the war and had settled for reasonable, if not all-that-could-be-wished-for, peace terms. Although none of the North Carolina delegates was centrally involved in the negotiation and ratification of the final peace agreement, Williamson, Hawkins, Blount, and Spaight were eager advocates of peace, exerting a positive influence, and Williamson's role, though not vital, was at times very important.

7

the north carolina delegates: an evaluation

THERE WAS NEVER a time during the Revolutionary War when North Carolina was represented by a great delegation in the Continental Congress, but this did not make North Carolina different from most of the other states. Only two states, Virginia and Massachusetts, were consistently represented by outstanding delegations, while New York, Pennsylvania, and South Carolina had better-than-ordinary delegations on occasion. The interesting fact is that the majority of delegates, regardless of which state they represented, were men of average ability. On the whole, they were dependable rather than dramatic and were noted more for their perseverance than for their initiative and imagination. Yet, most of the delegations contained at least one member as capable as the outstanding delegates from the states mentioned above. North Carolina was no exception, having its Thomas Burke, William Hooper, and Hugh Williamson.

Aside from the fact that most of its number were unexceptional men, the North Carolina delegation's performance lacked distinction for two major reasons—the provincialism of the delegates and the breakdown in communications between the delegates and the political leaders back home. There can be little doubt that too many of the North Carolina delegates were confirmed provincials. This did not keep them from winning respect as congressmen, for during the Revolution numerous members of Congress tended to have an overly provincial attitude. The flower of American nationalism was just beginning to bud, and men who wanted no more than a loose confederation of sovereign states were definitely in the majority. But the present crises of war and economic instability could not be shared and overcome by the states without creating among them a bond more meaningful than mere friendship. Sooner or later provincialism was almost certain, under the impact of interstate cooperation and mutual sacrifice, to lose ground to nationalism. Some of the true statesmen of the Revolution, including Thomas Burke, saw this before the war ended, and they began to think more in terms of American objectives than in terms of the narrow interests of their individual states. Burke, the fanatical state-sovereignty champion of 1777, was an eloquent spokesman for "all America" by 1780. From time to time some of the other North Carolina delegates elevated the American cause above the interests of their state, but most of the time a majority of the North Carolinians focused their attention on North Carolina's problems and showed scant concern for the larger cause. Such men drifted with prevailing tides, and most of them, though voicing a few mild objections, would have little difficulty accepting a new union with its more powerful central government after 1789. Some of them, like Hugh Williamson, Benjamin Hawkins, and Samuel Johnston, would even welcome it.

The provincialism of the North Carolina delegates is understandable. They were chosen by the North Carolina Provincial Congress (General Assembly after 1776), paid by that body, and subject to immediate recall if they took any action which that body regarded as detrimental to North Carolina's interests. Under such pressures, only extraordinary men would be more concerned about the needs of the American states as a whole than about the problems and wishes of North Carolina.

Even William Hooper, who would later come to see the need for a strong central government, was more concerned with gaining advantages for North Carolina during the Confederation debates. His protest against using population to determine tax quotas was clearly based on his chauvinistic judgment that, though populous, North Carolina was less able to pay taxes than other states of similar population. The state, he said, was a striking exception to the general rule "that the Riches of a Country are in Proportion to the Numbers of Inhabitants." The attitude that North Carolina should receive from Congress as much help as possible and contribute to Congress as little money as possible persisted during the war. It was again demonstrated in 1778 by Harnett's and Penn's great indignation over Congress's initial refusal to grant more than a portion of their state's request for financial assistance. Almost simultaneously Harnett was complaining about the amount of the tax quota Congress had assigned to North Carolina—and North Carolina's assessment was relatively small.

North Carolina's attitude naturally led to charges that the state was shirking its responsibilities; yet North Carolina's delegates always stood ready to defend their state's reputation, as illustrated by Hugh Williamson and William Blount in 1782. In a letter to Governor Martin on August 3, the two delegates reported that the "public papers" held up "to public Shame" the states which were "backward in performing their share of public service or in contributing their share towards the necessary expences of the War." North Carolina, they pointed out, had "long been viewed in a very unfavorable point of light." To offset the derogatory reports about North Carolina's efforts, Williamson and Blount had drafted and "caused to be published in the *Pennsylvania Journal* and *Packet*" a "Summary account" of what North Carolina had accomplished and contributed that year. According to their report to Governor Martin, they had stuck strictly to the truth and at the same time had produced "No unpleasing picture of our Country. . . ."

In spite of their sensitivity to slights against their state and their frequently selfish provincialism, there were times when it appeared that the North Carolina delegates might loose themselves from the bonds of narrow provincialism and act for the interest of the nation. For example, Harnett, protective of state interests as he usually was, condemned the "ridiculous jealousy" that marred attempts at cooperation between North Carolina and South Carolina. On behalf of the common cause he called upon his state to collect taxes to prevent "the ruin of the prodigious quantity of paper money . . . in Circulation." He wanted the various state legislatures to enact price controls because the "villanous practice of raising the price of all the Necessaries & Conveniences" was "spreading all over the Continent." The Wilmington merchant firmly believed that the United States, with the help of European allies, could triumph over Great Britain, but not unless each state did its share. He earnestly hoped that North Carolina would be cooperative by opening courts for the recovery of debts by creditors of other states, levying taxes like the other states, and calling in paper money issued under the authority of the Crown. Congress had recommended these steps, and, to Harnett, the existence of Americans as a free people depended upon his state and others taking them.

There were other signs that the delegates were beginning to have some regard for American interests. In the summer of 1779, when bankruptcy stared Congress squarely in the face, Thomas Burke and John Penn defended Congress's refusal to grant North Carolina's request for $2,500,000. They persuaded Congress to give $1,000,000 but then told Governor Caswell that they hoped the state would return some of it. Their sympathies, at least for the moment, were definitely with Congress, the symbol of the central government.

The North Carolina delegates sided with Congress on other occasions, also. In January, 1779, the North Carolina General Assembly instructed Burke, Penn, and Hill to support the nomination of North Carolina's Colonel Thomas Clark for brigadier general in the Continental Army. The three delegates voted as they were instructed, but to indicate their disagreement with the instructions, Burke and Hill refused to stand when they voted. Congress turned Clark down on the ground that another candidate had more seniority, and all three North Carolina delegates defended Congress's decision in their home state. Apparently the General Assembly did not take offense, for no one was recalled.

Despite the delegates' occasional displays of loyalty to the central government, there can be little doubt that loyalty to their state was far stronger. During the same month that they supported Congress in the Clark incident, the North Carolinians insisted that it was the right of their state and not of the Continental Army to deploy North Carolina's Continental troops. The fact is inescapable that most of North Carolina's delegates could never think for very long in anything larger than provincial terms. Nearly all of them were like Williamson, who on June 7, 1783, wrote: "There is no Place in Congress nor out of it, in which I shall willingly neglect the Interest of our State." Even though 1783 was Williamson's most outstanding year in Congress, he was somewhat distracted from promoting national interests by state concerns and personal business associated with his mercantile connections. Four years later Williamson would attend the convention which produced the present Constitution of the United States, and in 1788 he would fight for its adoption because he had come to believe that a stronger central government was needed. Nonetheless, the fact remains that at the end of the Revolutionary War he seemed much influenced by provincial and personal considerations.

The only North Carolina delegate who came to have a wider appreciation of nationalism during the war years was Burke. By 1781, and even earlier, his actions clearly indicated that his provincial outlook was changing. In February, 1781, he served on a committee with James Madison, Samuel Adams, and others, which recommended that Congress *order* Pennsylvania and Georgia to raise troops for a southern force under General Nathanael Greene. Apparently Burke supported this proposal, which called upon Congress to issue orders to two "sovereign" states. Earlier that month Burke had seconded a motion by John Witherspoon of New Jersey which provided for Congress to assume the authority "of superintending the commercial regulations of every State. . . ." This motion was too radical for most members of Congress and was therefore defeated. On the same day that Witherspoon's motion was voted down, Congress resolved to ask the states for power to levy a five per cent duty on imports coming into the United States, and the evidence suggests that Burke voted for it. But in April Burke left Congress forever. Returning to North Carolina, he was elected governor in June. With Burke gone, the North Carolina delegation returned, for the most part, to its provincial and largely unremarkable ways.

Besides their own narrow attitudes, the delegates were hampered, as was noted at the beginning of this chapter, by the absence of adequate communication with their state government. The General Assembly elected them and sent them off to Congress with only the most general instructions. Then, for a whole year, the delegates were virtually ignored by the legislators who had chosen them. Sincerely desiring to represent the wishes of their state government and fully aware of the consequences that might result from a wrong vote, the delegates wanted and requested specific instructions from the General Assembly, but rarely did they receive any. Since the real political power of

North Carolina was vested in the Assembly, there was pressing need for some line of communication between that body and North Carolina's representatives in Congress. But instead of being able to deal with the Assembly, the delegates could maintain contact with the state only through the all-but-powerless governor. Four men, Richard Caswell, Abner Nash, Thomas Burke, and Alexander Martin, occupied the office of governor at various times during the war years—and not one of the four kept the congressional delegates well informed about developments in the state. Oftentimes the governor hesitated to instruct the delegation without first conferring with the General Assembly, which was not in session much of the time. And so the delegates labored in faraway Philadelphia, waiting for instructions that arrived belatedly, or not at all.

Vexing as being cut off must have been for the delegates, they, as a rule, bore it with unusual patience. Perhaps they gave state leaders the benefit of the doubt because mail deliveries were slow and uncertain. As early as July 26, 1776, Congress had created a Continental postal system, including post roads and post riders from "Falmouth in New England to Savannah in Georgia," but the system was plagued with all sorts of problems throughout the war. Mail deliveries were sometimes threatened with interruption by enemy troops, inflation steadily drove postal rates to dizzy heights, and post riders were not always in as big a hurry to reach their destinations as they might have been. A letter sent by post from Philadelphia to North Carolina took twelve to eighteen days to arrive. From time to time the delegates would entrust dispatches to friends or acquaintances who were en route to North Carolina, and governors would do the same in sending letters to them, but this did not ensure a quick or even a certain delivery of the mail. Whether a letter was going interstate from Philadelphia to Halifax, North Carolina, or whether it was going intrastate from Halifax to New Bern, its delivery during the war was always in doubt. The delegates in Congress understood the situation, and this probably accounts in large measure for their patience.

The correspondence that passed between the North Carolina delegation and the various governors of the state reveals that both parties were anxious to hear regularly from each other. Some delegates did not correspond as faithfully with the governor as others, but on the whole they kept the governors better informed on national affairs than the governors kept them informed on state affairs. Military developments were given priority by the delegates, but many other important concerns were also reported. In June, 1777, when a lull in congressional business gave Burke and Penn some unexpected spare time, they reported to Governor Caswell that they had asked Congress to add a new battalion of North Carolina troops to the Continental Army. They also informed him that the enemy had retreated from New Brunswick, New Jersey. In addition, Penn wrote that Congress had agreed to defer certain interstate disputes in the interest of forming a union and, finally, he warned Caswell to watch out for profiteers who had purchased salt cheaply in Maryland with the idea of selling it at exorbitant prices in other states. So communicative was Penn that Caswell, who apparently disliked the Granville County lawyer, was puzzled. Prior to his departure for Philadelphia, Penn had declined to discuss public affairs with the governor. Referring to that unsatisfactory encounter in a letter to Burke, Caswell remarked: "Very little conversation passed between him and myself on public matters, for reasons known to himself and which you may perhaps form some conjecture of. . . ." In attempting to fulfill his congressional responsibilities, Penn appeared willing to forget whatever bad feelings he had had toward Caswell.

Both Burke and Penn remained faithful in their correspondence with the governor, as did their colleague Cornelius Harnett. He, too, conscientiously wrote Caswell, a longtime friend, of all significant developments in Congress and on the battlefield. Congressional decisions affecting North Carolina were quickly passed on to the governor, usually with the recommendation that he urge the General Assembly to receive them favorably. American military successes, such as General Horatio Gates's victory over General John Burgoyne near Saratoga, New York (October 17, 1777), were reported with obvious delight. British triumphs, such as General William Howe's victories at Brandywine (September 11, 1777) and Germantown (October 4, 1777) and his capture of Philadelphia (September 26, 1777), were recounted matter-of-factly and without undue alarm. Harnett and his colleagues could nearly always find something encouraging to report, even about British victories. For example, when Howe occupied Philadelphia, the North Carolina delegates sent word to Caswell that the British general's position was "critical," because he was far from his ships!

For as long as he served in Congress, Harnett kept Caswell apprised of all important developments, but the governor demonstrated no such diligence in responding. At first Harnett was bothered by Caswell's unresponsiveness. In January, 1778, he and Penn made it quite clear that they were annoyed about being kept in the dark on affairs in North Carolina. Nine months later they again complained about not hearing from Caswell. And the following month, October, Harnett, attempting once more to open up a line of communication with state leaders, pointed out to Caswell that Congress gave greater heed to the requests of a state's delegates if it was obvious that they spoke for the state's authorities. On October 4, he wrote:

As the General Assembly is to sit the next month, I could wish, with my colleagues, to receive their particular demands. We find from experience that requisitions from States come with much greater certainty of success through the channel of their Governors than by a bare requisition from the Delegates, not having an instruction from authority to produce. I therefore hope your Excellency will be attentive to this circumstance.

In spite of Harnett's coaxing, Caswell did not change his ways. In November, 1779, with Georgia in British hands and South Carolina under attack, the North Carolina delegates in Philadelphia remained uninformed about their state's preparations and needs. Thomas Burke, in a letter to Caswell, emphasized the fact that lack of information from state authorities made his and his colleagues' position in Congress awkward and disagreeable.

Of the North Carolina governors serving during the war years, Caswell is the one whose failure to keep in touch with the delegates is hardest to justify. He had been a congressional delegate himself. He served as governor from 1777 to 1780, a time which was relatively free from crises. There were periodic alarms, of course, and important matters, such as raising North Carolina's quota of troops for the Continental Army, to claim the governor's attention, but there was no military threat like the one that plagued North Carolina after Gates's defeat at Camden. Inflation was a problem, but it had not yet taken its heaviest toll. Caswell's successor, Abner Nash, and Nash's successor, Thomas Burke, can be excused for their failure to correspond with the congressional representatives on the ground that they were confronted with one crisis after another. Nash had to grapple with the extreme emergency of Cornwallis's invading army. Scarcely knowing what to do, Nash asked the General Assembly to create a board of war to advise him on military matters during the times when the Assembly was not in session. Although the Assembly created a board of war, and then a council extraordinary, to assist the governor, neither worked to his satisfaction, and he refused to serve another year as governor. One can easily understand why Nash had little correspondence with the congressional delegates.

When Nash stepped aside, Thomas Burke was elected governor. Burke had been at his new post for just four months when a Tory partisan, David Fanning, and his followers captured him and spirited him off to South Carolina. Paroled to James Island in Charleston Harbor, the North Carolina governor, believing rumors that some Tories intended to assassinate him, violated his parole and fled. Burke returned to North Carolina and resumed his duties as governor, but the vicious criticism of his honor for violating his parole contributed to his not being reelected governor in 1782. He withdrew to Tyaquin, where he died in December, 1783. In all probability he would have gained a greater reputation as an American political leader if he had survived to serve his country after the war. His death at age thirty-six was one of North Carolina's great tragedies of the Revolutionary era.

Constant occupation with thorny problems made it all but impossible for Nash and Burke to maintain a regular correspondence with the North Carolina delegation. Although the political chaos in the state continued into the two terms of Burke's successor, Alexander Martin, the danger from British military activities had passed. Martin, who never experienced the pressing circumstances of his two predecessors, could have communicated regularly with the delegates in Congress. He did not do so, and more than once during 1782 and 1783 Williamson, Hawkins, and Blount let the governor know that his negligence aggravated them. On October 22, 1782, Williamson and Blount emphasized in a letter to Martin that they had regularly reported to him "whether any new subject of intelligence occurred or not." They implied that he had not returned the courtesy.

Martin did not mend his uncommunicative ways, and the delegates became increasingly frustrated. In September, 1783, they

wrote the governor that they were "absolutely without information" on such important questions as what North Carolina was
doing about redeeming its quota of Continental money by allowing state taxes to be paid in that currency, as Congress had
requested. The Continental money thus collected was then cred-
ited to the state's account as payment for its share of the war
debt. They complained that they were "obliged to negative every
question" put to them "on the subject of Continental Money."
Moreover, they remained ignorant of what the last General Assembly had done, except for hearing that it had passed one law
opening a land office and another "emitting some money." Approximately three months later, on December 5, Williamson,
writing from Annapolis, Maryland, told his friend John Gray
Blount of Washington, North Carolina, that the delegates continued "in the usual Ignorance" of what was "going on in
N. Carolina." They had not even received word on whether or
not the General Assembly had met.

The governor finally wrote the delegates on December 8.
Stating that he had not had "immediate opportunities of con-
veyance," he insisted that he was "under necessity to decline returning" their "answers" as often as he "wished" or they
"expected." He had been further handicapped by the General
Assembly's failure to meet in October. Since there would be
no session until April, 1784, he was unable to do much about
answering the questions the delegates had raised. He was, however, able to report that the "different Treasurers" of the state
had gathered about a million and a half dollars in Continental
money, for which North Carolina could be given credit.

Apparently the letter of September, in which the delegates had
so strongly objected to being kept ignorant of North Carolina's
affairs, had not reached Martin when he wrote on December 8,
for it was not until January 21, 1784, that he made an effort to
deal with their specific objections. In his January letter the gov-

ernor sympathized with the delegates in their embarrassment over the "great default" in North Carolina's "Continental Accounts." He agreed that such behavior would "lessen the importance of the State," but to his "great regret" he could not "remedy the evil." Martin had Richard Caswell working on the public accounts in preparation for an inspection by the "Continental Comptroller," but he was convinced that nothing could be settled before the General Assembly sat again. He was sorry for the delay.

Perhaps the breakdowns in communication between North Carolina's delegates and the state's political leaders can best be explained in terms of adjustment to drastic change. The political instability that was an integral part of the Revolution made a period of trial and error inevitable. That the General Assembly and the various governors did not give adequate attention to informing and instructing the state's congressional delegation is indisputable. But at the same time it is understandable. The Assembly convened irregularly and, when in session, did not sit for extended periods. There was hardly any way, therefore, for that body to serve continuously in an advisory capacity to the governor, or to the delegates in Congress. Although this *modus operandi* frequently made North Carolina's Congressmen ineffective, it was in perfect accord with the state constitution of 1776, a constitution which several congressional delegates, including Burke and Harnett, had helped to write.

Quite clearly the General Assembly did not deliberately make life miserable for the men it sent to Congress. The legislators respected the delegates and praised them publicly from time to time for their "many great and important services." When Harnett pointed out that the annual election of only three men to Congress taxed the physical powers of the delegates, the legislators adopted his proposal to elect six men and require only three to be in service at any one time. Complaints of financial embarrassment from the delegates prompted the General Assembly in July, 1781, to authorize them to draw money from the Continental treasury "upon the faith and Credit" of North Carolina. This action would undoubtedly have solved their financial problems—if the General Assembly had taken more pains to see that the state's "faith and Credit" remained good in the eyes of those who kept watch over that treasury!

The legislators apparently felt that their constitutional responsibilities did not require them to keep in constant touch with the delegates or to remain in session to give them specific instructions on every issue. Since the delegates were sent to Congress to represent North Carolina to the best of their ability, let them do it. If their best was not good enough, they would know that when they were not reelected in the annual elections. Seemingly this was the attitude, for the General Assembly's commission to Ephraim Brevard (who died before he could begin his term), Samuel Johnston, William Sharpe, and Benjamin Hawkins, all elected in 1781, "authorized and impowered" them to represent North Carolina in Congress. They were "to sit and vote . . . upon all manner of matters at their discretion" unless they received "particular Instructions from the General Assembly" of the state. In a word, the North Carolina delegates were on their own. In view of the fact that the delegates wanted more instructions than the Assembly saw the need to send, it is remarkable that so few misunderstandings occurred.

In nine years, seventeen men—all well-to-do and all distinguished for one achievement or another in their home state—did what they could for North Carolina in the Continental Congress. For all the good that five of the delegates—and perhaps ten—did (Allen Jones, Abner Nash, and John Williams did too little to rate being mentioned as delegates in this story), they might just as well never have crossed the threshold of the congressional meeting halls. But the same thing can be said about numerous delegates from other states. Who, other than specialists in the history of the various states and students of the Continental Congress, are familiar with the names of delegates such as Joseph Spencer, James Sykes, Joseph Clay, George Plater, Samuel Holten, George Frost, James Kinsey, John Haring, Charles Humphreys, Daniel Lowry, Isaac Matte, and Meriwether Smith? North Carolina, like all the other states, sent some men to Congress who had few talents, some who had middling talents, and a very limited number who had many talents. The state was fortunate that at least a few of its representatives had vision and ability—and something more than a local political reputation—for those men kept North Carolina from being continuously overshadowed in Congress by the strong delegations of Virginia and Massachusetts. Thanks to Hooper in the early days, then Burke, and finally Williamson, North Carolina periodically enjoyed some status in the first American legislative body.

appendix I

DECLARATION OF INDEPENDENCE

In Congress, July 4, 1776
A Declaration by the Representatives of the United States
Of America, In Congress Assembled

When, in the Course of human events, it becomes necessary for one People to dissolve the political bands which have connected them with another, and to assume among the Powers of the earth, the separate and equal station to which the Laws of Nature and of Nature's God entitle them, a decent respect to the opinions of mankind requires that they should declare the causes which impel them to the separation.

We hold these truths to be self-evident, that all men are created equal, that they are endowed by their Creator with certain unalienable Rights, that among these are Life, Liberty, and the pursuit of Happiness. That to secure these rights, Governments are instituted among Men, deriving their just powers from the consent of the governed, That whenever any Form of Government becomes destructive of these ends, it is the Right of the People to alter or to abolish it, and to institute new Government, laying its foundation on such principles and organizing its powers in such form, as to them shall seem most likely to effect their Safety and Happiness. Prudence, indeed, will dictate that Governments long established should not be changed for light and transient causes; and accordingly all experience hath shown, that mankind are more disposed to suffer, while evils are sufferable, than to right themselves by abolishing the forms to which they are accustomed. But when a long train of abuses and usurpations, pursuing invariably the same Object evinces a design to reduce them under absolute Despotism, it is their right, it is their duty, to throw off such Government, and to provide new Guards for their future security. —Such has been the patient sufferance of these Colonies; and such is now the necessity which constrains them to alter their former Systems of Government. The history of the present King of Great Britain is a history of repeated injuries and usurpations, all having in direct object the establishment of an absolute Tyranny over these States. To prove this, let Facts be submitted to a candid world.

He has refused his Assent to Laws the most wholesome and necessary for the public good.

He has forbidden his Governors to pass Laws of immediate and pressing importance, unless suspended in their operation till his Assent should be obtained; and when so suspended, he has utterly neglected to attend to them.

He has refused to pass other Laws for the accommodation of large districts of people, unless those people would relinquish the right of Representation in the Legislature, a right inestimable to them and formidable to tyrants only.

He has called together legislative bodies at places unusual, uncomfortable, and distant from the depository of their Public Records, for the sole purpose of fatiguing them into compliance with his measures.

He has dissolved Representative Houses repeatedly, for opposing, with manly firmness his invasions on the rights of the people.

He has refused for a long time, after such dissolutions, to cause others to be elected; whereby the Legislative Powers, incapable of Annihilation, have returned to the People at large for their exercise; the State remaining, in the mean time exposed to all the dangers of invasion from without, and convulsions within.

He has endeavored to prevent the population of these States; for that purpose obstructing the Laws of Naturalization of Foreigners; refusing to pass others to encourage their migration hither, and raising the conditions of new Appropriations of Lands.

He has obstructed the Administration of Justice, by refusing his Assent to Laws for establishing Judiciary Powers.

He has made Judges dependent on his Will alone, for the tenure of their offices, and the amount and payment of their salaries.

He has erected a multitude of New Offices, and sent hither swarms of Officers to harass our People, and eat out their substance.

He has kept among us, in times of peace, Standing Armies without the Consent of our legislature.

He has affected to render the Military independent of and superior to the Civil Power.

He has combined with others to subject us to a jurisdiction foreign to our constitution, and unacknowledged by our laws; giving his Assent to their acts of pretended legislation:

For quartering large bodies of armed troops among us:

For protecting them, by a mock Trial, from Punishment for any Murders which they should commit on the Inhabitants of these States:

For cutting off our Trade with all parts of the world:

For imposing taxes on us without our Consent:

For depriving us in many cases, of the benefits of Trial by Jury:

For transporting us beyond Seas to be tried for pretended offences:

For abolishing the free System of English Laws in a neighboring province, establishing therein an Arbitrary government, and enlarging its Boundaries so as to render it at once an example and fit instrument for introducing the same absolute rule into these Colonies:

For taking away our Charters, abolishing our most valuable Laws, and altering fundamentally the Forms of our Governments:

For suspending our own Legislature, and declaring themselves invested with Power to legislate for us in all cases whatsoever.

He has abdicated Government here, by declaring us out of his Protection and waging War against us.

He has plundered our seas, ravaged our Coasts, burnt our towns, and destroyed the lives of our people.

He is at this time transporting large armies of foreign mercenaries to compleat the works of death, desolation and tyranny, already begun with circumstances of Cruelty & perfidy scarcely paralleled in the most barbarous ages, and totally unworthy the Head of a civilized nation.

He has constrained our fellow Citizens taken Captive on the high Seas to bear Arms against their Country, to become the executioners of their friends and Brethren, or to fall themselves by their Hands.

He has excited domestic insurrections amongst us, and has endeavoured to bring on the inhabitants of our frontiers, the merciless Indian Savages, whose known rule of warfare, is an undistinguished destruction of all ages, sexes and conditions.

In every stage of these Oppressions We have Petitioned for Redress in the most humble terms: Our repeated Petitions have been answered only by repeated injury. A Prince, whose character is thus marked by every act which may define a Tyrant, is unfit to be the ruler of a free People.

Nor have We been wanting in attention to our British brethren. We have warned them from time to time of attempts by their legislature to extend an unwarrantable jurisdiction over us. We have reminded them of the circumstances of our emigration and settlement here. We have appealed to their native justice and magnanimity, and we have conjured them by the ties of our common kindred to disavow these usurpations, which, would inevitably interrupt our connections and correspondence. They too have been deaf to the voice of justice and of consanguinity. We must, therefore, acquiesce in the necessity, which denounces our Separation, and hold them, as we hold the rest of mankind, Enemies in War, in Peace Friends.

We, therefore, the Representatives of the united States of America, in General Congress, Assembled, appealing to the Supreme Judge of the world for the rectitude of our intentions, do, in the Name, and by Authority of the good People of these Colonies, solemnly publish and declare, That these United Colonies are, and of Right ought to be Free and Independent States; that they are Absolved from all Allegiance to the British Crown, and that all political connection between them and the State of Great Britain, is and ought to be totally dissolved; and that as Free and Independent States, they have full Power to levy War, conclude Peace, contract Alliances, establish Commerce, and do all other Acts and Things which Independent States may of right do. And for the support of this Declaration, with a firm reliance on the Protection of Divine Providence, we mutually pledge to each other our Lives, our Fortunes, and our sacred Honor.

[The foregoing Declaration was, by order of Congress, engrossed, and signed by the following members:]

John Hancock

NEW HAMPSHIRE
Josiah Bartlett
Wm. Whipple
Matthew Thornton

MASSACHUSETTS-BAY
Saml. Adams
John Adams
Robt. Treat Paine
Elbridge Gerry

RHODE ISLAND
Step. Hopkins
William Ellery

NEW YORK
Wm. Floyd
Phil. Livingston
Frans. Lewis
Lewis Morris

PENNSYLVANIA
Robt. Morris
Benjamin Rush
Benja. Franklin
John Morton
Geo. Clymer
Jas. Smith
Geo. Taylor
James Wilson
Geo. Ross

VIRGINIA
George Wythe
Richard Henry Lee
Th. Jefferson
Benja. Harrison
Ths. Nelson, Jr.
Francis Lightfoot Lee
Carter Braxton

SOUTH CAROLINA
Edward Rutledge
Thos. Heyward, Junr.
Thomas Lynch, Junr.
Arthur Middleton

CONNECTICUT
Roger Sherman
Sam'el Huntington
Wm. Williams
Oliver Wolcott

NEW JERSEY
Richd. Stockton
Jno. Witherspoon
Fras. Hopkinson
John Hart
Abra. Clark

DELAWARE
Caesar Rodney
Geo. Read
Tho. M'Kean

MARYLAND
Samuel Chase
Wm. Paca
Thos. Stone
Charles Carroll of
    Carrollton

NORTH CAROLINA
Wm. Hooper
Joseph Hewes
John Penn

GEORGIA
Button Gwinnett
Lyman Hall
Geo. Walton

appendix II

THE CONSTITUTION OF NORTH CAROLINA,
December 18, 1776

A Declaration of Rights made by the Representatives of the Freemen of the State of North Carolina

I. That all Political Power is vested in and derived from the People only.

II. That the People of this State ought to have the sole and exclusive Right of regulating the internal Government and Police thereof.

III. That no man or Set of men, are intitled to exclusive or separate Emoluments or Privileges from the Community, but in Consideration of Public Services.

IV. That the legislative, executive and supreme judicial Powers of Government, ought to be forever separate and distinct from each other.

V. That all Power of suspending Laws, or the Execution of Laws, by any Authority, without Consent of the Representatives of People, is injurious to their Rights and ought not to be exercised.

VI. That Elections of members, to serve as Representatives in General Assembly, ought to be free.

VII. That in all Criminal Prosecutions every man has a Right to be informed of the accusation against him, and to confront the Accusers and Witnesses with other Testimony, and shall not be compelled to give Evidence against himself.

VIII. That no Freeman shall be put to answer any Criminal Charge, but by Indictment, Presentment or Impeachment.

IX. That no Freeman shall be convicted of any crime, but by the unanimous verdict of a Jury of good and lawful men, in open Court as heretofore used.

X. That excessive Bail should not be required, nor excessive Fines imposed, nor cruel or unusual punishment inflicted.

XI. That General Warrants, whereby any Officer or Messenger may be commanded to search suspected Places, without Evidences of the Fact committed, or to seize any Person or Persons not named, whose Offence is not particularly described and supported by Evidence, are dangerous to Liberty, and ought not to be granted.

XII. That no Freeman ought to be taken, imprisoned or disseized of his Freehold, Liberties, or Privileges, or outlawed or exiled, or in any manner destroyed or deprived of his Life, Liberty, or Property, but by the Law of the Land.

XIII. That every Freeman restrained of his Liberty is intitled to a Remedy to enquire into the Lawfulness thereof, and to remove the same if unlawful, and that such Remedy ought not to be denied or delayed.

XIV. That in all Controversies at Law respecting property, the ancient Mode of Trial by Jury is one of the best Securities of the Rights of the People, and ought to remain sacred and Inviolable.

XV. That the Freedom of the Press is one of the great Bulwarks of Liberty, and therefore ought never to be restrained.

XVI. That the People of this State ought not to be taxed or made subject to the Payment of any Impost or Duty, without the Consent of themselves or their Representatives in General Assembly freely given.

XVII. That the People have a Right to bear Arms for the Defence of the State, and as Standing Armies in Time of Peace are dangerous to Liberty, they ought not to be kept up, and that the military should be kept under strict Subordination to, and governed by the Civil Power.

XVIII. That the People have a Right to assemble together, to consult for their common Good, to instruct their Representatives, and to apply to the Legislature for Redress of Grievances.

XIX. That all men have a natural and unalienable right to worship Almighty God according to the dictates of their own consciences.

XX. That for redress of grievances and for amending and strengthening the laws, elections ought to be often held.

XXI. That a frequent recurrence to fundamental principles is absolutely necessary to preserve the blessings of liberty.

XXII. That no hereditary emoluments, privileges or honours ought to be granted or conferred in this State.

XXIII. That perpetuities and monopolies are contrary to the genius of a free State, and ought not to be allowed.

XXIV. That retrospective laws punishing acts committed before the existence of such laws, and by them only declared criminal, are oppressive, unjust and incompatible with liberty, wherefore no *ex post facto* law ought to be made.

XXV. The property of the soil in a free government being one of the essential rights of the collective body of the people, it is necessary, in order to avoid future disputes that the limits of the State should be ascertained with precision; . . . [hereafter follows a description of North Carolina boundaries] beginning on the sea side at a cedar stake, at or near the mouth of Little River . . .

Therefore all the Territory, Seas, Waters, and Harbours, with their appurtenances, lying between the Line above described and the Southern Line of the State of Virginia, which begins on the Sea Shore, in thirty six Degrees thirty Minutes North Latitude, and from thence runs West agreeable to the said Charter of King Charles, are the Right and Property of the People of this State, to be held by them in Sovereignty: any partial Line, without the consent of the Legislature of this State, at any Time thereafter directed or laid out in any wise, notwithstanding. Provided always, That this Declaration of Rights shall not prejudice any Nation or Nations of Indians from enjoying such hunting Grounds as may have been, or hereafter shall be secured to them, by any former or future Legislature of this State. And provided also, That it shall not be construed so as to prevent the Establishment of one or more Governments Westward of this State, by the consent of the Legislature. And provided further, That nothing herein contained shall effect the Titles or Possessions of Individuals, holding or claiming under the Laws heretofore in force or Grants heretofore made by the late King George III or his Predecessors or the late Lords Proprietors, or any of them.

December the Seventeenth, one Thousand Seven Hundred and Seventy Six, read the third time, and ratified in open Congress.

R^d CASWELL, President.

JAS. GREEN, Junr, Sec'y.

———

The Constitution or Form of Government, agreed to and resolved upon by the Representatives of the Freemen of the State of North Carolina, elected and Chosen for that particular Purpose in Congress assembled, at Halifax, the Eighteenth Day of December, in the year of our Lord One Thousand Seven Hundred and Seventy Six.

Whereas Allegiance and Protection are in their Nature reciprocal and the one should of Right be refused, when the other is withdrawn; and whereas George the Third, King of Great Britain, and late Sovereign of the British American Colonies, hath not only withdrawn from them his Protection, but by an Act of the British Legislature declared the Inhabitants of these States out of the Protection of the British Crown, and all their property found upon the High Seas liable to be seized and confiscated to the Uses mentioned in the said Act. And the said George the Third has also sent Fleets and Armies to prosecute a cruel war against them, for the Purpose of reducing the Inhabitants of the said Colonies to a State of abject Slavery, in consequence whereof, all Government under the said King within the said Colonies hath ceased, and a total Dissolution of Government in many of them hath taken Place.

And whereas, the Continental Congress having considered the Premises, and other previous Violations of the Rights of the good People of America, have therefore declared, that the Thirteen United Colonies are of Right wholly absolved from all Allegiance to the British Crown, or any other foreign jurisdiction whatsoever; and that the said Colonies now are, and forever shall be, free and independent States. Wherefore, in our present State, in order to prevent Anarchy and confusion, it becomes necessary that Government should be established in this State; therefore, we, the Representatives of the Freemen of North Carolina, chosen and assembled in Congress for the express Purpose of framing a Constitution under the authority of the People, most conducive to their Happiness and Prosperity, do declare that a Government for this State shall be established in manner and Form following, to wit:

I. That the legislative Authority shall be vested in two distinct Branches, both dependent on the People, to wit, a Senate and House of Commons.

II. That the Senate shall be composed of Representatives annually chosen by Ballot, one from each County in the State.

III. That the House of Commons shall be composed of Representatives annually chosen by Ballot, two for each County, and one for each of the Towns of Edenton, Newbern, Wilmington, Salisbury, Hillsborough, and Halifax.

IV. That the Senate and House of Commons, assembled for the Purpose of Legislation, shall be denominated the General Assembly.

V. That each member of the Senate shall have usually resided in the County in which he is chosen for one year immediately preceding his Election, and for the same time shall have possessed, and continue to possess, in the County which he represents, not less than Three Hundred Acres of Land in Fee.

VI. That each member of the House of Commons shall have usually resided in the County in which he is chosen for one year immediately preceding his Election, and for six months shall have possessed, and continue to possess, in the County which he represents, not less than One Hundred Acres of Land in Fee or for the Term of his own Life.

VII. That all Freemen of the age of Twenty One Years, who have been Inhabitants of any one County within the State twelve months immediately preceding the Day of any Election and possessed of a Freehold within the same County of Fifty Acres of Land for six months next before, and at the Day of Election, shall be entitled to vote for a member of the Senate.

VIII. That all Freemen of the Age of Twenty One Years who have been Inhabitants of any county within the State twelve months immediately preceding the Day of any Election, and shall have paid Public Taxes, shall be intitled to vote for members of the House of Commons for the county in which he resides.

IX. That all Persons possessed of a Freehold in any Town in this State, having a Right of Representation, and also all Freemen who have been Inhabitants of any such Town twelve months next before, and at the Day of Election, and shall have paid Public Taxes, shall be intitled to vote for a member to represent such Town in the House of Commons: Provided always, That this Section shall not intitle any Inhabitant of such Town to vote for members of the House of Commons for the County in which he may reside, nor any Freeholder in such County who resides without, or beyond the limits of such Town, to vote for a member for said Town.

X. That the Senate and House of Commons, when met, shall each have Power to choose a Speaker, and other their Officers, be Judges of the Qualifications and Elections of their members, sit upon their own Adjournments from Day to Day, and prepare Bills to be passed in Laws. The two Houses shall direct Writs of Election for supplying intermediate Vacancies, and shall also jointly, by Ballot, adjourn themselves to any Future Day and Place.

XI. That all Bills shall be read three Times in each House before they pass into Laws, and be signed by the Speaker of both Houses.

XII. That every Person who shall be chosen a member of the Senate or House of Commons or appointed to any Office or Place of Trust, before taking his Seat, or entering upon the Execution of his Office, shall take an Oath to the State, and all Officers shall also take an Oath of Office.

XIII. That the General Assembly shall, by joint ballot of both Houses, appoint Judges of the Supreme Courts of Law and Equity, Judges of Admiralty, and Attorney General, who shall be commissioned by the Governor and hold their offices during good behaviour.

XIV. That the Senate and House of Commons shall have power to appoint the Generals and Field Officers of the Militia, and all officers of the regular army of this State.

XV. That the Senate and House of Commons, jointly at their first meeting after each annual election, shall by ballot elect a Governor for one year, who shall not be eligible to that office longer than three years in six successive years. That no person under 30 years of age, and who has not been a resident in this State above 5 years, and having in the State a freehold in lands and tenements above the value of one thousand pounds, shall be eligible as Governor.

XVI. That the Senate and House of Commons, jointly, at their first meeting after each annual election, shall by ballot elect seven persons to be a Council of State for one year, who shall advise the Governor in the execution of his office, and that four members shall be a quorum; their advice and proceedings, shall be entered into a Journal to be kept for that purpose only, and signed by the members present, to any part of which any member present may enter his dissent. And such Journal shall be laid before the General Assembly, when called for by them.

XVII. That there shall be a Seal of this State, which shall be kept by the Governor, and used by him as occasion may require; and shall be called the Great Seal of the State of North Carolina, and be affixed to all grants and commissions.

XVIII. The Governor for the time being, shall be Captain General and Commander in Chief of the Militia, and in the recess of the General Assembly, shall have power, by and with the advice of the Council of State, to embody the militia for the public safety.

XIX. That the Governor, for the Time being, shall have power to draw for and apply such sums of money as shall be voted by the General Assembly for the Contingencies of Government, and be accountable to them for the same. He also may, by and with the Advice of the Council of State, lay Embargoes, or prohibit the Exportation of any Commodity, for any Term not exceeding thirty Days at any one Time, in the Recess of the General Assembly; and shall have the Power of granting Pardons and Reprieves, except where the Prosecution shall be carried on by the General Assembly, or the Law shall otherwise direct, in which case he may, in the Recess, grant a Reprieve until the next sitting of the General Assembly; and may exercise all the other executive Powers of Government, limited and restrained as by this Constitution is mentioned, and according to the Laws of the State. And on his Death, Inability or Absence from the State, the Speaker of the Senate for the Time being, and in Case of his Death, Inability or Absence from the State, the Speaker of the House of Commons, shall exercise the Powers of Governor after such death, or during such Absence or Inability of the Governor or Speaker of the Senate, or until a new nomination is made by the General Assembly.

XX. That in every case where any Officer, the Right of whose appointment is by this Constitution vested in the General Assembly, shall, during their Recess, die, or his Office by other means become vacant, the Governor shall have Power, with the Advice of the Council of State, to fill up such vacancy, by granting a temporary Commission, which shall expire at the end of the next Session of the General Assembly.

XXI. That the Governor, Judges of the Supreme Court of Law and Equity, Judges of Admiralty, and Attorney General shall have adequate Salaries during their Continuance in Office.

XXII. That the General Assembly shall, by joint Ballot of both Houses, annually appoint a Treasurer or Treasurers for this State.

XXIII. That the Governor and other Officers offending against the State, by violating any Part of this Constitution, Mal-Administration, or Corruption, may be prosecuted on the Impeachment of the General Assembly, or Presentment of the Grand Jury of any Court of Supreme Jurisdiction in this State.

XXIV. That the General Assembly shall, by joint Ballot of both Houses, triennially appoint a Secretary for this State.

XXV. That no Persons who heretofore have been or hereafter

may be Receivers of Public Monies, shall have a Seat in either House of General Assembly, or be eligible to any Office in this State, until such Person shall have fully accounted for and paid into the Treasury all Sums for which they may be accountable and liable.

XXVI. That no Treasurer shall have a seat in either Senate, House of Commons, or Council of State during his continuance in that Office, or before he shall have finally settled his Accounts with the Public for all Monies which may be in his hands at the Expiration of his Office, belonging to the State, and hath paid the same into the Hands of the succeeding Treasurer.

XXVII. That no Officer in the regular Army or Navy in the Service and Pay of the United States of this or any other State, nor any Contractor or Agent for supplying such Army or Navy with Clothing or Provisions, shall have a seat in either the Senate or House of Commons or Council of State, or be eligible thereto; and any Member of the Senate, House of Commons, or Council of State, being appointed to, and accepting of such Office, shall thereby vacate his seat.

XXVIII. That no Member of the Council of State shall have a seat either in the Senate or House of Commons.

XXIX. That no Judge of the Supreme Court of Law or Equity, or Judge of Admiralty, shall have a seat in the Senate, House of Commons, or Council of State.

XXX. That no Secretary of this State, Attorney General, or Clerk of any Court of Record, shall have a seat in the Senate, House of Commons, or Council of State.

XXXI. That no Clergyman or Preacher of the Gospel, of any Denomination, shall be capable of being a member either of the Senate, House of Commons or Council of State, while he continues in the Exercise of the Pastoral Function.

XXXII. That no person who shall deny the Being of God, or the Truth of the Protestant Religion, or the divine Authority either of the Old or New Testament, or shall hold religious Principles incompatible with the Freedom and Safety of the State, shall be capable of holding any Office, or Place of Trust or Profit, in the civil Department within this State.

XXXIII. That the Justices of the Peace within their respective Counties in this State, shall in future be recommended to the Governor, for the Time being, by the Representatives in General Assembly, and the Governor shall commission them accordingly; and the Justices, when so commissioned, shall hold their Offices during good Behaviour, and shall not be removed from Office by the General Assembly, unless for Misbehaviour, Absence, or Inability.

XXXIV. That there shall be no Establishment of any one religious Church or Denomination in this State in Preference to any other, neither shall any person, on any pretence whatsoever, be compelled to attend any Place of worship contrary to his own Faith or Judgment, or be obliged to pay for the Purchase of any Glebe, or the building of any House of Worship, or for the maintenance of any Minister or Ministry, contrary to what he believes right, or has voluntarily and personally engaged to perform, but all persons shall be at Liberty to exercise their own mode of Worship. Provided, That nothing herein contained shall be construed to exempt Preachers of treasonable and seditious Discourses, from legal trial and Punishment.

XXXV. That no person in the State shall hold more than one lucrative Office at any one Time. Provided, That no appointment in the Militia, or the Office of a Justice of the Peace, shall be considered as a lucrative Office.

XXXVI. That all Commissions and Grants shall run in the name of the State of North Carolina and bear Test, and be signed by the Governor. All writs shall run in the same manner, and bear Test, and be signed by the Clerks of the respective Courts. Indictments shall conclude, Against the Peace and Dignity of the State.

XXXVII. That the Delegates from this State to the Continental Congress, while necessary, shall be chosen annually by the General Assembly, by Ballot, but may be superseded in the mean time in the same manner, and no person shall be elected to serve in that Capacity for more than three years successively.

XXXVIII. That there shall be a Sheriff, Coroner, or Coroners, and Constable, in each County in this State.

XXXIX. That the person of a Debtor, where there is not a strong Presumption of Fraud, shall not be continued in Prison, after delivering up, *bona fide*, all his Estate, real and personal, for the Use of his Creditors, in such manner as shall be hereafter regulated by Law. All prisoners shall be bailable by sufficient sureties, unless for Capital Offences, when the proof is evident, or Presumption great.

XL. That every Foreigner who comes to settle in this State, having first taken the Oath of Allegiance to the same, may purchase, or by other just means acquire, hold and transfer, Land, or other real Estate; and after one year's Residence, shall be deemed a free citizen.

XLI. That a school or schools be established by the Legislature, for the convenient Instruction of youth, with such Salaries to the Masters, paid by the Public as may enable them to instruct at low prices; and all useful Learning shall be duly encouraged and promoted in one or more Universities.

XLII. That no purchase of lands shall be made of the Indian natives, but on behalf of the public, by the authority of the General Assembly.

XLIII. That the future Legislature of this State shall regulate intails, in such a manner as to prevent perpetuities.

XLIV. That the declaration of rights is hereby declared to be part of the Constitution of this State, and ought never to be violated on any pretence whatsoever.

XLV. That any member of either House of the General Assembly shall have liberty to dissent from, and protest against any act or resolve which he may think injurious to the public, or any individual, and have the reasons of his dissent entered on the Journals.

XLVI. That neither House of the General Assembly shall proceed upon public business, unless a majority of all the members of such House are actually present, and that upon a motion made and seconded, the yeas and nays upon any question shall be taken and entered on the Journals; and that the Journals of the proceedings of both Houses of the General Assembly shall be printed and made public, immediately after their adjournment.

This Constitution is not intended to preclude the present Congress from making a temporary provision for the well ordering of this State, until the General Assembly shall establish Government agreeable to the mode herein before described.

December the Eighteenth, One Thousand Seven Hundred and Seventy Six, read the third time, and ratified in open Congress.

RICHARD CASWELL, President.

By order   JAMES GREEN, JUN., Sec'ry.

appendix III

THE ARTICLES OF CONFEDERATION

Agreed to by Congress November 15, 1777;
Ratified and in force, March 1, 1781

To ALL TO WHOM these Presents shall come, we the undersigned Delegates of the States affixed to our Names send greeting. Whereas the Delegates of the United States of America in Congress assembled did on the fifteenth day of November in the Year of our Lord One Thousand Seven Hundred and Seventy seven, and in the Second Year of the Independence of America agree to certain articles of Confederation and perpetual Union between the States of New-hampshire, Massachusetts-bay, Rhodeisland and Providence Plantations, Connecticut, New York, New Jersey, Pennsylvania, Delaware, Maryland, Virginia, North-Carolina, South-Carolina and Georgia in the Words following, viz. "Articles of Confederation and perpetual Union between the states of Newhampshire, Massachusetts-bay, Rhodeisland and Providence Plantations, Connecticut, New-York, New-Jersey, Pennsylvania, Delaware, Maryland, Virginia, North-Carolina, South-Carolina and Georgia.

ART. I. The Stile of this confederacy shall be "The United States of America."

ART. II. Each state retains its sovereignty, freedom and independence, and every Power, Jurisdiction and right, which is not by this confederation expressly delegated to the United States, in Congress assembled.

ART. III. The said states hereby severally enter into a firm league of friendship with each other, for their common defence, the security of their Liberties, and their mutual and general welfare, binding themselves to assist each other, against all force offered to, or attacks made upon them, or any of them, on account of religion, sovereignty, trade, or any other pretence whatever.

ART. IV. The better to secure and perpetuate mutual friendship and intercourse among the people of the different states in this union, the free inhabitants of each of these states, paupers, vagabonds and fugitives from Justice excepted, shall be entitled to all privileges and immunities of free citizens in the several states; and the people of each state shall have free ingress and regress to and from any other state, and shall enjoy therein all the privileges of trade and commerce, subject to the same duties, impositions and restrictions as the inhabitants thereof respectively, provided that such restriction shall not extend so far as to prevent the removal of property imported into any state, to any other state of which the Owner is an inhabitant; provided also that no imposition, duties or restriction shall be laid by any state, on the property of the united states, or either of them.

If any Person guilty of, or charged with treason, felony, or other high misdemeanor in any state, shall flee from Justice, and be found in any of the united states, he shall upon demand of the Governor or executive power, of the state from which he fled, be delivered up and removed to the state having jurisdiction of his offence.

Full faith and credit shall be given in each of these states to the records, acts and judicial proceedings of the courts and magistrates of every other state.

Art. V. For the more convenient management of the general interests of the united states, delegates shall be annually appointed in such manner as the legislature of each state shall direct, to meet in Congress on the first Monday in November, in every year, with a power reserved to each state, to recall its delegates, or any of them, at any time within the year, and to send others in their stead, for the remainder of the Year.

No state shall be represented in Congress by less than two, nor by more than seven Members; and no person shall be capable of being a delegate for more than three years in any term of six years; nor shall any person, being a delegate, be capable of holding any office under the united states, for which he, or another for his benefit receives any salary, fees or emolument of any kind.

Each state shall maintain its own delegates in a meeting of the states, and while they act as members of the committee of the states.

In determining questions in the united states, in Congress assembled, each state shall have one vote.

Freedom of speech and debate in Congress shall not be impeached or questioned in any Court, or place out of Congress, and the members of congress shall be protected in their persons from arrests and imprisonments, during the time of their going to and from, and attendance on congress, except for treason, felony, or breach of the peace.

ART. VI. No state without the Consent of the united states in congress assembled, shall send any embassy to, or receive any embassy from, or enter into any conference, agreement, or alliance or treaty with any King, prince or state; nor shall any person holding any office of profit or trust under the united states, or any of them, accept of any present, emolument, office or title of any kind whatever from any king, prince or foreign state; nor shall the united states in congress assembled, or any of them, grant any title of nobility.

No two or more states shall enter into any treaty, confederation or alliance whatever between them, without the consent of the united states in congress assembled, specifying accurately the purposes for which the same is to be entered into, and how long it shall continue.

No state shall lay any imposts or duties, which may interfere with any stipulations in treaties, entered into by the united states in congress assembled, with any king, prince or state, in pursuance of any treaties already proposed by congress, to the courts of France and Spain.

No vessels of war shall be kept up in time of peace by any state, except such number only, as shall be deemed necessary by the united states in congress assembled, for the defence of such state, or its trade; nor shall any body of forces be kept up by any state, in time of peace, except such number only, as in the judgment of the united states, in congress assembled, shall be deemed requisite to garrison the forts necessary for the defence of such state; but every state shall always keep up a well regulated and disciplined militia, sufficiently armed and accoutred, and shall provide and constantly have ready for use, in public stores, a due number of field pieces and tents, and a proper quantity of arms, ammunition and camp equipage.

No state shall engage in any war without the consent of the united states in congress assembled, unless such state be actually invaded by enemies, or shall have received certain advice of a resolution being formed by some nation of Indians to invade such state, and the danger is so imminent as not to admit of a delay, till the united states in congress assembled can be consulted: nor shall any state grant commissions to any ships or vessels of war, nor letters of marque or reprisal, except it be after a declaration of war by the united states in congress assembled, and then only against the kingdom or state and the subjects thereof, against which war has been so declared, and under such regulations as shall be established by the united states in congress assembled, unless such state be infested by pirates, in which case vessels of war may be fitted out for that occasion, and kept so long as the danger shall continue, or until the united states in congress assembled shall determine otherwise.

ART. VII. When land-forces are raised by any state for the common defence, all officers of or under the rank of colonel, shall be appointed by the legislature of each state respectively by whom such forces shall be raised, or in such manner as such state shall direct, and all vacancies shall be filled up by the state which first made the appointment.

ART. VIII. All charges of war, and all other expences that shall be incurred for the common defence or general welfare, and allowed by the united states in congress assembled, shall be defrayed out of a common treasury, which shall be supplied by the several states, in proportion to the value of all land within each state, granted to or surveyed for any Person, as such land and the buildings and improvements thereon shall be estimated according to such mode as the united states in congress assembled, shall from time to time direct and appoint. The taxes for paying that proportion shall be laid and levied by the authority and direction of the legislatures of the several states within the time agreed upon by the united states in congress assembled.

ART. IX. The united states in congress assembled, shall have the sole and exclusive right and power of determining on peace and war, except in the cases mentioned in the sixth article—of sending and receiving ambassadors—entering into treaties and alliances, provided that no treaty of commerce shall be made whereby the legislative power of the respective states shall be restrained from imposing such imposts and duties on foreigners, as their own people are subjected to, or from prohibiting the exportation or importation of any species of goods or commodities whatsoever—of establishing rules for deciding in all cases, what captures on land or water shall be legal, and in what manner prizes taken by land or naval forces in the service of the united states shall be divided or appropriated—of granting letters of marque and reprisal in time of peace—appointing courts for the trial of piracies and felonies committed on the high seas and establishing courts for receiving and determining finally appeals in all cases of captures, provided that no member of congress shall be appointed a judge of any of the said courts.

The united states in congress assembled shall also be the last resort on appeal in all disputes and differences now subsisting or that hereafter may arise between two or more states concerning boundary, jurisdiction or any other cause whatever; which authority shall always be exercised in the manner following. Whenever the legislative or executive authority or lawful agent of any state in controversy with another shall present a petition to congress stating the matter in question and praying for a hearing, notice thereof shall be given by order of congress to the legislative or executive authority of the other state in controversy, and a day assigned for the appearance of the parties by their lawful agents, who shall then be directed to appoint by joint consent, commissioners or judges to constitute a court for hearing and determining the matter in question: but if they cannot agree, congress shall name three persons out of each of the united states, and from the list of such persons each party shall alternately strike out one, the petitioners beginning, until the number shall be reduced to thirteen; and from that number not less than seven, nor more than nine names as congress shall direct, shall in the presence of congress be drawn out by lot, and the persons whose names shall be so drawn or any five of them, shall be commissioners or judges, to hear and finally determine the controversy, so always as a major part of the judges who shall hear the cause shall agree in the determination: and if either party shall neglect to attend at the day appointed, without shewing reasons, which congress shall judge sufficient, or being present shall refuse to strike, the congress shall proceed to nominate three persons out of each state, and the secretary of congress shall strike in behalf of such party absent or refusing; and the judgment and sentence of the court to be appointed, in the manner before prescribed, shall be final and conclusive; and if any of the parties shall refuse to submit to the authority of such court, or to appear to defend their claim or cause, the court shall nevertheless proceed to pronounce sentence, or judgment, which shall in like manner be final and decisive, the judgment or sentence and other proceedings being in either case transmitted to congress, and lodged among the acts of congress for the security of the parties concerned: provided that every commissioner, before he sits in judgment, shall take an oath to be administered by one of the judges of the supreme or superior court of the state, where the cause shall be tried, "well and truly to hear and determine the matter in question, according to the best of his judgment, without favour, affection or hope of reward:" provided also that no state shall be deprived of territory for the benefit of the united states.

All controversies concerning the private right of soil claimed under different grants of two or more states, whose jurisdictions as they may respect such lands, and the states which passed such grants are adjusted, the said grants or either of them being at the same time claimed to have originated antecedent to such settlement of jurisdiction, shall on the petition of either party to the congress of the united states, be finally determined as near as may be in the same manner as is before prescribed for deciding disputes respecting territorial jurisdiction between different states.

The united states in congress assembled shall also have the sole and exclusive right and power of regulating the alloy and value of coin struck by their own authority, or by that of the respective states—fixing the standard of weights and measures throughout the united states.—regulating the trade and managing all affairs with the Indians, not members of any of the states, provided that the legislative right of any state within its own limits be not infringed or violated—establishing and regulating post-offices from one state to another, throughout all the united states, and exacting such postage on the papers passing thro' the same as may be requisite to defray the expences of the said office—appointing all officers of the land forces, in the service of the united states, excepting regimental officers.—appointing all the officers of the naval forces, and commissioning all officers whatever in the service of the united states—making rules for the government and regulation of the said land and naval forces, and directing their operations.

The united states in congress assembled shall have authority to appoint a committee, to sit in the recess of congress, to be denominated "A Committee of the States," and to consist of one delegate from each state; and to appoint such other committees and civil officers as may be necessary for managing the general affairs of the united states under their direction—to appoint one of their number to preside, provided that no person be allowed to serve in the office of president more than one year in any term of three years; to ascertain the necessary sums of Money to be raised for the service of the united states, and to appropriate and apply the same for defraying the public expences—to borrow money, or emit bills on the credit of the united states, transmitting every half year to the respective states an account of the sums of money so borrowed or emitted,—to build and equip a navy—to agree upon the number of land forces, and to make requisitions from each state for its quota, in proportion to the number of white inhabitants in such state; which requisition shall be binding, and thereupon the legislature of each state shall appoint the regimental officers, raise the men and cloath, arm and equip them in a soldier like manner, at the expence of the united states, and the officers and men so cloathed, armed and equipped shall march to the place appointed, and within the time agreed on by the united states in congress assembled: But if the united states in congress assembled shall, on consideration of circumstances judge proper that any state should not raise men, or should raise a smaller number than its quota, and that any other state should raise a greater number of men than the quota thereof, such extra number shall be raised, officered, cloathed, armed and equipped in the same manner as the quota of such state, unless the legislature of such state shall judge that such extra number cannot be safely spared out of the same, in which case they shall raise officer, cloath, arm and equip as many of such extra number as they judge can be safely spared. And the officers and men so cloathed, armed and equipped, shall march to the place appointed, and within the time agreed on by the united states in congress assembled.

The united states in congress assembled shall never engage in a war, nor grant letters of marque and reprisal in time of peace, nor enter into any treaties or alliances, nor coin money, nor regulate the value thereof, nor ascertain the sums and expences necessary for the defence and welfare of the united states, or any of them, nor emit bills, nor borrow money on the credit of the united states, nor appropriate money, nor agree upon the number of vessels of war, to be built or purchased, or the number of land or sea forces to be raised, nor appoint a commander in chief of the army or navy, unless nine states assent to the same: nor shall a question on any other point, except for adjourning from day to day be determined, unless by the votes of a majority of the united states in congress assembled.

The congress of the united states shall have power to adjourn to any time within the year, and to any place within the united states, so that no period of adjournment be for a longer duration than the space of six Months, and shall publish the Journal of their proceedings monthly, except such parts thereof relating to treaties, alliances or military operations as in their judgment require secresy; and the yeas and nays of the delegates of each state on any question shall be entered on the Journal, when it is desired by any delegate; and the delegates of a state, or any of them, at his or their request shall be furnished with a transcript of the said Journal, except such parts as are above excepted, to lay before the legislatures of the several states.

ART. X. The committee of the states, or any nine of them, shall be authorised to execute, in the recess of congress, such of the powers of congress as the united states in congress assembled, by the consent of nine states, shall from time to time think expedient to vest them with; provided that no power be delegated to the said committee, for the exercise of which, by the articles of confederation, the voice of nine states in the congress of the united states assembled is requisite.

ART. XI. Canada acceding to this confederation, and joining in the measures of the united states, shall be admitted into, and entitled to all the advantages of this union: but no other colony shall be admitted into the same, unless such admission be agreed to by nine states.

ART. XII. All bills of credit emitted, monies borrowed and debts contracted by, or under the authority of congress, before the assembling of the united states, in pursuance of the present confederation, shall be deemed and considered as a charge against the united states, for payment and satisfaction whereof the said united states, and the public faith are hereby solemnly pledged.

ART. XIII. Every state shall abide by the determinations of the united states in congress assembled, on all questions which by this confederation are submitted to them. And the Articles of this confederation shall be inviolably observed by every state, and the union shall be perpetual; nor shall any alteration at any time hereafter be made in any of them; unless such alteration be agreed to in a congress of the united states, and be afterwards confirmed by the legislatures of every state.

AND WHEREAS it hath pleased the Great Governor of the World to incline the hearts of the legislatures we respectively represent in congress, to approve of, and to authorize us to ratify the said articles of confederation and perpetual union. KNOW YE that we the undersigned delegates, by virtue of the power and authority to us given for that purpose, do by these presents, in the name and in behalf of our respective constituents, fully and entirely ratify and confirm each and every of the said articles of confederation and perpetual union, and all and singular the matters and things therein contained: And we do further solemnly plight and engage the faith of our respective constituents, that they shall abide by the determinations of the united states in congress assembled, on all questions, which by the said confederation are submitted to them. And that the articles thereof shall be inviolably observed by the states we respectively represent, and that the union shall be perpetual. In Witness whereof we have hereunto set our hands in Congress. Done at Philadelphia in the state of Pennsylvania the ninth Day of July in the year of our Lord one Thousand seven Hundred and Seventy-eight, and in the third year of the independence of America.

On the part and behalf of the State of:

NEW HAMPSHIRE
Josiah Bartlett
John Wentworth, Jun[r]
August 8th 1778

RHODE-ISLAND
and
PROVIDENCE
PLANTATIONS
William Ellery
Henry Marchant
John Collins

NEW JERSEY
Jno Witherspoon
Nath[l] Scudder
Nov[r] 26, 1778

MARYLAND
John Hanson
March 1 1781
Daniel Carroll d[o]

PENNSYLVANIA
Rob[t] Morris
Daniel Roberdeau
Jon[a] Bayard Smith
William Clingan
Joseph Reed
22[d] July 1778

VIRGINIA
Richard Henry Lee
John Banister
Thomas Adams
Jn[o] Harvie
Francis Lightfoot
    Lee

NEW YORK
Ja[s] Duane
Fra[s] Lewis
W[m] Duer
Gouv Morris

N⁰ CAROLINA
John Penn July 21st 1778
Corn^s Harnett
Jn° Williams

SOUTH-CAROLINA
Henry Laurens
William Henry
   Drayton
Jn° Mathews
Richd Hutson
Thos Heyward Junr

CONNECTICUT
Roger Sherman
Samuel Huntington
Oliver Wolcott
Titus Hosmer
Andrew Adams

MASSACHUSETTS BAY
John Hancock
Samuel Adams
Elbridge Gerry
Francis Dana
James Lovell
Samuel Holten

DELAWARE
Tho M:Kean Feby 12 1779
John Dickinson
May 5th 1779
Nicholas Van Dyke

GEORGIA
Jn° Walton 24th
   July 1778
Edwd Telfair
Edwd Langworthy

appendix IV

TREATY OF PARIS

Paris, September 3, 1783
Peace Treaty between Great Britain and
the United States of America

In the name of the Most Holy and Undivided Trinity.

It having pleased the Divine Providence to dispose the hearts of the most serene and most potent Prince George the Third, by the Grace of God King of Great Britain, France, and Ireland, Defender of the Faith, Duke of Brunswick and Luneberg, Arch-Treasurer and Prince Elector of the Holy Roman Empire, &ca., and of the United States of America, to forget all past misunderstandings and differences that have unhappily interrupted the good correspondence and friendship which they mutually wish to restore; and to establish such a beneficial and satisfactory intercourse between the two countries, upon the ground of reciprocal advantages and mutual convenience, as may promote and secure to both perpetual peace and harmony: And having for this desirable end already laid the foundation of peace and reconciliation, by the provisional articles, signed at Paris, on the 30th of Nov'r, 1782, by the commissioners empowered on each part, which articles were agreed to be inserted in and to constitute the treaty of peace proposed to be concluded between the Crown of Great Britain and the said United States, but which treaty was not to be concluded until terms of peace should be agreed upon between Great Britain and France, and His Britannic Majesty should be ready to conclude such treaty accordingly; and the treaty between Great Britain and France having since been concluded, His Britannic Majesty and the United States of America, in order to carry into full effect the provisional articles above mentioned, according to the tenor thereof, have constituted and appointed, that is to say, His Britannic Majesty on his part, David Hartley, esqr., member of the Parliament of Great Britain; and the said United States on their part, John Adams, esqr., late a commissioner of the United States of America at the Court of Versailles, late Delegate in Congress from the State of Massachusetts, and chief justice of the said State, and Minister Plenipotentiary of the said United States to their High Mightinesses the States General of the United Netherlands; Benjamin Franklin, esq're, late Delegate in Congress from the State of Pennsylvania, president of the convention of the said State, and Minister Plenipotentiary from the United States of America at the Court of Versailles; John Jay, esq're, late president of Congress, and chief justice of the State of New York, and Minister Plenipotentiary from the said United States at the Court of Madrid, to be the Plenipotentiaries for the concluding and signing the present definitive treaty; who, after having reciprocally communicated their respective full powers, have agreed upon and confirmed the following articles:

ART. I. His Britannic Majesty acknowledges the said United States, viz. New Hampshire, Massachusetts Bay, Rhode Island, and Providence Plantations, Connecticut, New York, New Jersey, Pennsylvania, Delaware, Maryland, Virginia, North Carolina, South Carolina, and Georgia, to be free, sovereign and independent States; that he treats with them as such, and for himself, his heirs and successors, relinquishes all claims to the Government, proprietary and territorial rights of the same, and every part thereof.

ART. II. And that all disputes which might arise in future, on the subject of the boundaries of the said United States may be prevented, it is hereby agreed and declared, that the following are, and shall be their boundaries, viz.: From the northwest angle of Nova Scotia, viz.: that angle which is formed by a line drawn due north from the source of Saint Croix River to the Highlands; along the said Highlands which divide those rivers that empty themselves into the river St. Lawrence, from those which fall into the Atlantic Ocean, to the northwesternmost head of the Connecticut River; thence down along the middle of that river, to the forty-fifth degree of north latitude; from thence, by a line due west on said latitude, until it strikes the river Iroquois or Cataraquy; thence along the middle of said river into Lake Ontario, through the middle of said lake until it strikes the communication by water between that lake and Lake Erie; thence along the middle of the said communication into Lake Erie, through the middle of said lake until it arrives at the water communication between that lake and Lake Huron; thence along the middle of said water communication into the Lake Huron; thence through the middle of said lake to the water communication between that lake and Lake Superior; thence through Lake Superior northward of the Isles Royal and Phelipeaux, to the Long Lake; thence through the middle of said Long Lake, and the water communication between it and the Lake of the Woods, to the said Lake of the Woods; thence through the said lake to the most northwestern point thereof, and from thence on a due west course to the river Mississippi; thence by a line to be drawn along the middle of the said river Mississippi until shall intersect the northernmost part of the thirty-first degree of north latitude. South, by a line to be drawn due east from the determination of the line last mentioned, in the latitude of thirty-one degrees north of the Equator, to the middle of the river Appalachicola or Catahouche; thence along the middle thereof to its junction with the Flint River; thence straight to the head of St. Mary's River; and thence down along the middle of St. Mary's River to the Atlantic Ocean. East, by a line to be drawn along the middle of the river St. Croix, from its mouth in the Bay of Fundy to its source, and from its source directly north to the aforesaid Highlands, which divide the rivers that fall into the Atlantic Ocean from those which fall into the river St. Lawrence; comprehending all islands within twenty leagues of any part of the shores of the United States, and lying between lines to be drawn due east from the points where the aforesaid boundaries between Nova Scotia on the one part, and East Florida on the other, shall respectively touch the Bay of Fundy and the Atlantic Ocean; excepting such islands as now are, or heretofore have been, within the limits of the said province of Nova Scotia.

ART. III. It is agreed that the people of the United States shall continue to enjoy unmolested the right to take fish of every kind on the Grand Bank, and on all the other banks of Newfoundland; also in the Gulph of Saint Lawrence, and at all other places in the sea where the inhabitants of both countries used at any time heretofore to fish. And also that the inhabitants of the United States shall have liberty to take fish of every kind on such part of the coast of Newfoundland as British fishermen shall use (but not to dry or cure the same on that island) and also on the coasts, bays and creeks of all other of His Britannic Majesty's dominions in America; and that the American fishermen shall have liberty to dry and cure fish in any of the unsettled bays, harbours and creeks of Nova Scotia, Magdalen Islands, and Labrador, so long as the same shall remain unsettled; but so soon as the same or either of them shall be settled, it shall not be lawful for the said fishermen to dry or cure fish at such settlements, without a previous agreement for that purpose with the inhabitants, proprietors or possessors of the ground.

ART. IV. It is agreed that creditors on either side shall meet with no lawful impediment to the recovery of the full value in sterling money, of all *bona fide* debts heretofore contracted.

ART. V. It is agreed that the Congress shall earnestly recommend it to the legislatures of the respective States, to provide for the restitution of all estates, rights and properties which have been confiscated, belonging to real British subjects, and also of the estates, rights and properties of persons resident in districts in the possession of His Majesty's arms, and who have not borne arms against the said United States. And that persons of any other description shall have free liberty to go to any part or parts of any of the thirteen United States, and therein to remain twelve months, unmolested in their endeavours to obtain the restitution of such of their estates, rights and properties as may have been confiscated; and that Congress shall also earnestly recommend to the several States a reconsideration and revision of all acts or laws regarding the premises, so as to render the said laws or acts perfectly consistent, not only with justice and equity, but with that spirit of conciliation which, on the return of the blessings of peace, should universally prevail. And that Congress shall also earnestly recommend to the several States, that the estates, rights and properties of such last mentioned persons, shall be restored to them, they refunding to any persons who may be now in possession, the *bona fide* price (where any has been given) which such persons may have paid on purchasing any of the said lands, rights or properties, since the confiscation. And it is agreed, that all persons who have any interest in confiscated lands, either by debts, marriage settlements or otherwise, shall meet with no lawful impediment in the prosecution of their just rights.

ART. VI. That there shall be no future confiscations made, nor any prosecutions commenced against any person or persons for, or by reason of the part which he or they may have taken in the present war; and that no person shall, on that account, suffer any future loss or damage, either in his person, liberty or property; and that those who may be in confinement on such charges, at the time of the ratification of the treaty in America, shall be immediately set at liberty, and the prosecutions so commenced be discontinued.

ART. VII. There shall be a firm and perpetual peace between His Britannic Majesty and the said States, and between the subjects of the one and the citizens of the other, wherefore all hostilities, both by sea and land, shall from henceforth cease; All prisoners on both sides shall be set at liberty, and His Britannic Majesty shall, with all convenient speed, and without causing any destruction, or carrying away any negroes or other property of the American inhabitants, withdraw all his armies, garrisons and fleets from the said United States, and from every post, place and harbour within the same; leaving in all fortifications the American artillery that may be therein: And shall also order and cause all archives, records, deeds and papers, belonging to any of the said States, or their citizens, which, in the course of the war, may have fallen into the hands of his officers, to be forthwith restored and deliver'd to the proper States and persons to whom they belong.

ART. VIII. The navigation of the river Mississippi, from its source to the ocean, shall forever remain free and open to the subjects of Great Britain, and the citizens of the United States.

ART. IX. In case it should so happen that any place or territory belonging to Great Britain or to the United States, should have been conquer'd by the arms of either from the other, before the arrival of the said provisional articles in America, it is agreed, that the same shall be restored without difficulty, and without requiring any compensation.

ART. X. The solemn ratification of the present treaty, expedited in good and due form, shall be exchanged between the contracting parties, in the space of six months, or sooner if possible, to be computed from the day of the signature of the present treaty. In witness whereof, we the undersigned, their Ministers Plenipotentiary, have in their name and in virtue of our full powers, signed with our hands the present definitive treaty, and caused the seals of our arms to be affix'd thereto.

Done at Paris, this third day of September, in the year of our Lord one thousand seven hundred and eighty-three.

Seal   D. Hartley
Seal   John Adams
Seal   B. Franklin
Seal   John Jay

bibliography

I. PRIMARY SOURCES

A. Manuscript Collections

In gathering material for this book the authors have examined all pertinent manuscript collections in the following depositories: Boston Public Library, Library of Columbia University, Library of Congress, Connecticut Historical Society, Library of Duke University, Historical Society of Pennsylvania, Massachusetts Historical Society, National Archives, New York Historical Society, New York Public Library, North Carolina Department of Archives and History, Pierpont Morgan Library, Library of the University of North Carolina.

B. Printed Sources

The following represent a small sample of the published primary sources upon which the authors have drawn:

Adams, Charles F., ed., *The Works of John Adams, Second President of the United States: With a Life of the Author*, 10 volumes. Boston: Little, Brown, and Company, 1850–1856.

Boyd, Julian P., ed., *The Papers of Thomas Jefferson*, in process of publication. Princeton University Press, 1950 to date.

Burnett, Edmund C., ed., *Letters of Members of the Continental Congress*, 8 volumes. Washington: Carnegie Institution of Washington, 1921–1936.

Butterfield, Lyman H., ed., *Diary and Autobiography of John Adams*, 4 volumes. Cambridge, Mass.: The Belknap Press, 1961.

——, ed., *Letters of Benjamin Rush*, 2 volumes. Princeton: Princeton University Press, 1951.

Force, Peter, and M. St. Clair Clarke, eds., *American Archives: A Documentary History of the English Colonies in North America*, 6 volumes. Fourth and Fifth Series. Washington: Clark and Force, 1837–1846.

Ford, Worthington C. and others, eds., *Journals of the Continental*

Congress, 1774–1789, 34 volumes. Washington: Government Printing Office, 1904–1937.

Hunt, Gaillard, ed., *The Writings of James Madison*, 9 volumes. New York: G. P. Putnam's Sons, 1900–1910.

McRee, Griffith J., ed., *Life and Correspondence of James Iredell, One of the Associate Justices of the Supreme Court of the United States*, 2 volumes. New York: D. Appleton and Company, 1857–1858.

Sparks, Jared, ed., *The Diplomatic Correspondence of the American Revolution*, 12 volumes. Boston: N. Hale, Gray and Bowen, 1829–1830.

Stevens, Benjamin F., ed., *Facsimilies of Manuscripts in European Archives Relating to America, 1773–1783*, 25 volumes. London: Malby and Sons, 1889–1895.

Wharton, Francis, ed., *The Revolutionary Diplomatic Correspondence of the United States*, 6 volumes. Washington: Government Printing Office, 1889.

In addition to the above, the authors carefully perused the contemporary North Carolina and Pennsylvania newspapers.

II. SECONDARY SOURCES

The authors used a very long list of secondary works, including monographs, biographies, and articles. A select number of those that were most helpful follows:

Abernethy, Thomas P., *Western Lands and the American Revolution*. New York: D. Appleton-Century Company, 1937.

Alden, John R., *The South in the Revolution, 1763–1789*. Baton Rouge: Louisiana State University Press, 1957.

Ashe, Samuel A., *History of North Carolina*, 2 volumes. Greensboro and Raleigh: Charles L. Van Noppen, 1908 and 1925.

Bemis, Samuel F., *The Diplomacy of the American Revolution*. Bloomington: Indiana University Press, 1957.

Bezanson, Anne, *Prices and Inflation During the American Revolution, Pennsylvania, 1770–1790*. Philadelphia: University of Pennsylvania Press, 1951.

Bolles, Albert S., *The Financial History of the United States, from 1774–1789*. New York: D. Appleton and Company, 1879.

Burnett, Edmund C., *The Continental Congress*. New York: The Macmillan Company, 1941.

Connor, Robert D. W., *History of North Carolina*, 6 volumes. Chicago and New York: The Lewis Publishing Company, 1919.

Crittenden, Charles C., *The Commerce of North Carolina, 1763–1789*. New Haven: Yale University Press, 1936.

East, Robert A., *Business Enterprise in the American Revolutionary Era*. New York: Columbia University Press, 1938.

Ferguson, E. James, *The Power of the Purse: A History of American Public Finance, 1776–1790*. Chapel Hill: University of North Carolina Press, 1961.

Friedenwald, Herbert, *The Declaration of Independence*. New York: The Macmillan Company, 1904.

Hazelton, John H., *The Declaration of Independence*. New York: Dodd, Mead and Company, 1906.

Henderson, H. James, *Party Politics in the Continental Congress*. New York: McGraw-Hill, 1974.

Jensen, Merrill, *The Articles of Confederation: An Interpretation of the Social-Constitutional History of the American Revolution, 1774–1781*. Madison: University of Wisconsin Press, 1959.

————, *The New Nation: A History of the United States During the Confederation, 1781–1789*. New York: Alfred A. Knopf, 1958.

Lefler, Hugh T., and Albert Ray Newsome, *North Carolina: The History of a Southern State*. Revised Edition. Chapel Hill: University of North Carolina Press, 1963.

McGee, Dorothy H., *Famous Signers of the Declaration*. New York: Dodd, Mead and Company, 1955.

MacMillan, Margaret B., *The War Governors in the American Revolution*. New York: Columbia University Press, 1943.

Main, Jackson T., *The Antifederalists: Critics of the Constitution, 1781–1788*. Chapel Hill: University of North Carolina Press, 1961.

————, *Political Parties Before the Constitution*. Chapel Hill: published for the Institute of Early American History and Culture at Williamsburg, Va., by the University of North Carolina Press, 1973.

Montross, Lynn, *The Reluctant Rebels: The Story of the Continental Congress, 1774–1789*. New York: Harper and Brothers, 1950.

Morrill, James R., *The Practice and Politics of Fiat Finance: North*

Carolina in the Confederation. Chapel Hill: University of North Carolina Press, 1969.

Morris, Richard B., *The Peacemakers: The Great Powers and American Independence.* New York: Harper & Row, 1965.

Nevins, Allan, *The American States During and After the Revolution, 1775–1789.* New York: The Macmillan Company, 1924.

Rankin, Hugh F., *The North Carolina Continentals.* Chapel Hill: University of North Carolina Press, 1971.

Sanders, Jennings B., *Evolution of Executive Departments of the the Continental Congress, 1774–1789.* Chapel Hill: University of North Carolina Press, 1935.

————, *The Presidency of the Continental Congress, 1774–1789: A Study in American Institutional History.* Chicago: University of Chicago Press, 1930.

Schlesinger, Arthur M., Sr., *The Colonial Merchants and the American Revolution, 1763–1775.* New York: Frederick Ungar Publishing Company, 1957. (Published originally in 1918.)

Wood, Gordon S., *The Creation of the American Republic, 1776– 1787.* Chapel Hill: published for the Institute of Early American History and Culture at Williamsburg, Va., by the University of North Carolina Press, 1969.

In addition to the works listed above, plus numerous biographies and articles which are not listed, the authors found two special works very helpful. They are:

Greene, Evarts B., and Virginia D. Harrington, *American Population Before the Federal Census of 1790.* New York: Columbia University Press, 1932.

Lord, Clifford, *Atlas of Congressional Roll Calls.* Cooperstown: Publisher Unknown, 1943. Located in the Brown University Library.

index

Adams, John, 6, 9, 10, 37, 38, 85, 92

Adams, Samuel, 101; "the Sam Adams of North Carolina," 41–42

American liberties, 18, 19, 26

Anglo-American commercial relations, 7, 16, 20, 89–92, 93–94

Annapolis, Md., 107

Articles of Confederation: Burke's opposition to, 42, 46, 48–99; debates about, 39–40; Harnett's support of, 46–49; Maryland's delay in ratification of, 49, 73–74; representation of states under, 4; taxation provisions of (Article VIII), 67, 75, 77–78, 92; voting provisions of, 5, 92. *See also* Confederation of states

Backcountry of North Carolina, 13, 61

Baltimore, Md., 31, 35, 39, 44

Blount, John Gray, 88, 92, 107

Blount, Thomas, 88

Blount, William, 65, 86, 93, 95; cession plan of, 78; correspondence of, 77, 85, 88, 98, 106; evaluation of, 66

Board of War (in Congress), 28, 63

Brandywine, Battle of, 44, 104

Brevard, Ephraim, 109

Bunker Hill, Battle of, 3

Burgoyne, General John, 104

Burke, Thomas, 31, 56, 59, 62, 65, 103; advocacy of states' rights, 36–40, 48–49, 97; attitude toward finances, 51–53, 99; attitude toward western lands, 74, 75, 77; Constitution of North Carolina written by, 35, 42, 108; early life of, 35–36; growing nationalism of, 100, 101; prestige of, 27, 40, 50, 66, 96, 110; relations with North Carolina delegation, 41–42, 43–44, 46; service as governor, 102, 105, 106; work for peace, 84–85

Camden, Battle of, 59, 61, 105

Canada, 18, 84

Carpenter's Hall, 10n

Caswell, Richard: as delegate to Congress, 3, 7–9, 12, 17–18; as governor, 40, 102–4; as leader of the Patriots, 20; as Treasurer of North Carolina, 13, 108; background of, 5, 14; correspondence of, 44, 46, 49, 52, 56, 58, 74, 99

Central government, 36–37, 40, 90, 98, 99, 100

Cession Act (North Carolina, 1784), 82

Charleston, S.C., 58, 63, 65; James Island, in harbor of, 106
Cherokee War of 1776, 61, 78
Chowan County, 53
Clark, Colonel Thomas, 100
Committee, of Congress, 10, 12, 24n, 61, 65, 66; on American diplomatic agents, 94; on New York's western claims, 74–75; on preliminary peace objectives, 84; on South Carolina's government, 18–19
Committee of Secret Correspondence (actually a standing board), 28
Committees of safety (North Carolina), 4
Communications problems between the North Carolina delegates and state government, 43, 101–2, 104–9
Confederation of states (union), 103; attitudes of North Carolina delegates toward, 36–37, 39, 42–49; Congress of, 50, 82, 83; debates about, 36, 39–40, 44–46, 98; North Carolina's opposition to, 18, 49
Congress (Continental and Confederation), 20, 22, 32, 35, 36, 61, 78, 96, 101–10 passim; confederation issue in, 36–40, 42, 44–50, 73, 77; financial policies of, 45, 51–53, 55, 63–65, 66–67, 71, 98, 99, 101; First, 5–7, 18; independence decided in, 24–25; organization of, 3–5, 10–12, 27, 38–39, 65; peace negotiations of, 84–90, 92–95; postal system created by, 102; Second, 7–13, 18–19; temporary relocation of, 31, 38, 39, 44, 68, 104; war conducted by, 26–28, 50, 56, 58, 62–63, 68–70, 100
Congressional Journals, 37

Connecticut, 6, 47n, 73
Constitution of North Carolina (1776), 4, 27, 28, 30; framers of, 35
Constitution of the United States (1787), 4, 32, 83
Continental Army (Continental Line), 12, 44, 63, 80, 100, 103; composition of, 55–56, 58, 105; deserters from, 37–38; mutiny threatened in, 66, 68–70
Cornwallis, Lord Charles, 58, 62, 63, 75, 84, 105
Council extraordinary (North Carolina), 105
Council of State (proposed), 40
Cumberland River, 81

Davidson County, N.C. (in the "Tennessee Country"), 81
Davie, William R., 82
Dean, Silas, 6
Debt. See Money
Declaration of Independence, 2, 25, 28, 32
Delaware, 8, 73, 85
Democracy, 19, 25–26, 30, 61
Deserters. See Continental Army
Dickinson, John, 39
Disagreements on minor matters among North Carolina delegates, 14–16, 27–28, 40–41, 43, 44–46

Edenton, N.C., 7, 27, 28, 65
England (Great Britain and British Empire): attitudes of North Carolinians toward, 14, 16–21, 24–26, 30, 85–86; colonial policies of, 3, 20, 41–42; economic sanctions against, 7, 16, 32; military moves of, 44, 49, 58–59, 63, 104, 105; peace negotiations with, 84–85, 88–92, 93–95

Enlistment bounties, 56, 58
Executive (or standing) boards in Congress, 2, 10, 12, 24n, 28, 65

Fanning, David, 106
Financial problems. *See* Money
Fishing rights off Canada, 84–86
Foreign alliances, 20, 24, 28, 36–37, 50
Foreign loans, 63, 66
France, 66, 86–87, 92

Gates, General Horatio, 58–59, 61, 104–5
General Assembly of North Carolina (legislature), 40, 52, 93, 104–9 *passim*; attitude toward western land of, 74–75, 78–79, 81–82; election and control of delegates to Congress by, 4, 27–28, 56, 65, 97, 100, 101–2; payment of delegates by, 62; political battles in, 31–32; views about confederation of, 47–49
General Council (proposed), 40
George III, 17, 18, 20, 24
Georgia, 73, 101, 105
Germantown, Battle of, 104
Gerry, Elbridge, 94
Gilman, John Taylor, 87
Granville County, N.C., 13
Great Britain. *See* England
Greene, General Nathanael, 101

Halifax, N.C., 4, 8, 22, 27, 30, 35, 102
Halifax Resolves, 22–24
Harnett, Cornelius, 36, 40, 103–4; as state leader, 3, 41–42, 108; relations with North Carolina delegates, 43; views on confederation, 44–49, 99; views on finances, 53, 58; views on western land, 74, 98
Harvey, John, 3

Hawkins, Benjamin, 65, 97, 106, 109; accomplishments of, 66, 95; attitude toward western lands, 79; correspondence of, 68–70, 87, 89–90, 92
Henry, Patrick, 6
Hewes, Joseph, 3, 5, 30, 32, 40–41; as an agent of the Secret Committee, 27–28; as a delegate, 5, 9–10, 12, 14–20, 24–27; as a state leader, 7, 13–14, 19
Hill, Whitmel, 51–53, 59, 61, 62, 100
Hillsborough, N.C., 4, 13, 32, 35, 49
Hogg, James, 14–15
Hooper, William, 3, 22, 35, 42, 50, 66, 96; as a delegate, 6–9, 12–14, 16, 17–20, 28, 98, 110; conservatism of, 25–26, 30–32; early life of, 5–6, 14; service after Congress, 32
Howe, General William, 104

Illnesses of North Carolina delegates, 9, 13, 27, 35, 41–42
Independence, 16–20, 22, 24–26, 28, 50, 86, 95
Inflation, 50, 61, 69, 105
Iredell, James, 7, 13, 25, 55

Jay, John, 85
Jefferson, Thomas, 25, 65
Johnston, Samuel, 20, 61; as a delegate, 53, 55, 85, 97, 109
Johnston County, N.C., 5
Jones, Willie, 59, 61, 62, 74, 75

Knox, General Henry, 63

Laurens, Henry, 75
Laurens, John, 75
Lee, Arthur, 86
Lee, Charles, 12
Lee, Richard Henry, 6, 24, 37

Lillington, Alexander, 20
Loan certificates, 51–52
Loyalists, 20, 89

Madison, James, 62, 94, 101
Marine Naval Board, 10, 12, 24n, 27, 28
Martin, Alexander, 93–94, 102, 106; letters of, 80–82, 107–8; reports from delegates to, 66–70, 77–80, 85, 90, 95, 98
Martin, Josiah, 3, 6
Martin County, N.C., 51
Maryland, 8, 62, 71, 85, 103; delays ratification of Articles of Confederation, 49, 73–74
Massachusetts, 18, 41; delegates of, 9, 85, 94, 96, 110; legislature of, 3
McDonald, General Donald, 20
Military equipment, 26, 50, 55, 62, 63
Militias, 56, 61–63
Ministers of England, 17–18, 89–92
Mississippi River, 84–85
Money, 10, 12, 19, 27; Congress's efforts to raise, 45, 50–53, 55, 63, 66–71, 84; for use as enlistment bounties, 55–56, 58; North Carolina's actions regarding, 61–62, 69–70, 81–82, 99, 107–9
Moore's Creek Bridge, Battle of, 20
Morris, Robert, 42, 55, 63, 66, 68

Nash, Abner, 62–63, 75, 102, 105, 106, 109
Nationalism, 97, 99, 101
Naval stores, 7
Navigation Acts (British), 92
Navigation rights on Mississippi River, 84–85
New Bern, N.C., 3, 4, 27, 32, 40, 102

New Englanders, 46, 85
New Hampshire, 73, 85, 87
New Jersey, 73, 101
New York (state), 73, 80, 85, 96, 104
North, Lord Frederick, 18, 89, 90, 92
North Carolina delegates (as a group), 36, 42–43, 67, 82–83; attitudes toward peace negotiations of, 85–87, 90, 92–93, 95; communication problems of, 101–8; evaluation of, 96; financial problems of, 61–62, 69–70, 109; general responsibilities of, 3–5; life in Philadelphia of, 9–10, 12–16, 109; nationalism of, 99–100; positions on finance of, 51–52; positions on relations with England of, 17–20, 22, 24–28; positions on western land of, 45, 73–74, 78–79; provincialism of, 97–99, 100–1

Orange County, N.C., 48
Oswald, Richard, 88
Otis, James, 5

Paris, France, 89, 95
Patriots (North Carolina), 20
Peace with England, 68; commissioners to negotiate, 85, 86, 88; negotiations for, 84–86, 87–95; objectives of, 84–85, 94; treaty of (Treaty of Paris), 89, 90, 92, 94, 95
Pendleton, Edmund, 13
Penn, John, 18, 26, 31, 32, 58, 98–104 *passim*; actions in state politics of, 19, 22, 27–28, 56; attitude toward independence of, 20, 24–25; background of, 13–14; relations with North Carolina delegation of, 14–16, 40–41, 43, 44–46, 48

Pennsylvania, 42, 44, 49, 73, 96, 101; delegates from, 6, 37, 90

Pennsylvania Journal and *Packet*, 98

Philadelphia, Pa., college of, 65; Congress temporarily relocated from, 31, 38, 39, 44, 68, 104; cost of living in, 62; merchants of, 90; mentioned, 4–10, 13–18, 24–25, 27–28, 40–41, 55, 66, 85, 102, 103

Politics in North Carolina, 19, 27–28, 30–31, 101–2, 104–9; east-west division in, 13–15; leaders in, 20, 42, 47–49, 55, 61

Population figures, 7, 8, 47n

Postal system, 102–3

Presbyterians, 26

Princeton, N.J., 68

Prisoners of war, 85–86, 106

Provincial assembly (North Carolina), 3, 7

Provincial Congresses of North Carolina: First, 3; Second, 4, 5; Third, 4, 13, 14, 18; Fourth, 4, 22, 24, 25; Fifth, 4, 27, 28, 30, 35

Provincial council (North Carolina), 4

Provisional government (North Carolina), 4, 13

Quincy, Josiah, Jr., 41

Ratification of the Treaty of Paris. *See* Peace with England

Recruitment of soldiers, 50, 55–56, 58

Regulator Movement, 13–14, 19

Revolutionary War (war), 3, 9, 27, 36–37, 50, 96, 98; conclusion of, 74, 84, 95, 100; years of, 86, 102

Rhode Island, 67, 73, 77

Rush, Benjamin, 6

Salaries of North Carolina delegates, 4, 61–62, 69–70, 109

Savannah, Ga., 58

Secret Committee, 10, 27, 28

Sectionalism in North Carolina, 13–16

"1776," 24n

Sharpe, William, 59, 61–63, 74, 109

Sherman, Roger, 39

Shippen family, 16

Simes, Thomas, 26n

Smith, Robert, 27

Social activities of delegates, 9, 16

Sons of Liberty, 41

South Carolina, 8, 18–19, 56, 58, 73, 96, 99, 106

Spaight, Richard Dobbs, 2, 93, 95

Stamp Act (1765), 35, 41

Standing boards. *See* Executive boards

State-of-Prisoners Board, 28

State sovereignty, 36–39, 44, 45, 48, 97

Taxation, 44, 51, 52–53, 66, 71, 98; impost method of, 45, 67, 77, 101; in North Carolina, 82; proposed systems of, 45–48; under Article VIII, 67, 77–78, 82

Tennessee ("Tennessee Country" of North Carolina), 73, 75, 78, 79, 81, 83

Tories, 49, 106

Toryism, 25

Transylvania, 14–15

Treasury Board, 10, 27, 28

Tryon, William, 14

Tyaquin, 35, 106

Union. *See* Confederation.

Virginia, 8, 56, 61; delegates of, 24–25, 62, 86, 94, 96, 101, 110; western lands of, 73, 74, 79, 80

Washington, General George, 44, 55, 63, 68, 84

West Indies, 7, 12; British, 90, 92–94; French, 65, 87

Western lands, 44; as source of revenue, 71, 76–79; claimed by various states, 73; debated in Congress, 45, 74–75; settled by North Carolinians, 14–15, 79–84

Whig elitism, 14, 25, 30

Wilkinson, William, 46

Williamson, Hugh, 96, 97, 106–7, 110; arrival in Congress of, 65–67; attitude toward North Carolina of, 98–99, 100; financial problems of, 69–70; opinion regarding peace negotiations, 85–90, 92–95; position on western lands, 77–80, 82

Wilmington, N.C., 5, 7, 41, 49; British occupation of, 32, 63

Wilson, James, 37–39

Witherspoon, the Reverend John, 26, 101

York, Pa., 44

Yorktown, Va., 63, 71, 84